TEACHING CAN KILL YOU
HOW TO SURVIVE AND BE HAPPE
IN THE CLASSROOM

Sheryl A. Shields

Teaching Can Kill You: How to Survive and BE HAPPE in the Classroom

Published by Hamlin Street Press

Editor: Heidi Jo Wayco-Berden
Cover and interior design: FiveJsDesign.com

TABLE OF CONTENTS

Sherese and Stanten: This book would not have been possible without your constant love, support and encouragement. I'm eternally grateful for all you do or have done to help me live a truly Happe life.

FORWARD

I CREATED THIS BOOK BECAUSE I'VE BEEN BURNED OUT, frazzled and extremely frustrated. It was only after talking to hundreds of teachers who have experienced a school year from hell that I realized I needed to share their experiences and find solutions to the problems teachers face every single day.

Here's a small glimpse of what they have experienced:

Mary, a 10-year veteran and her fellow teachers voted unanimously to strike two weeks before school started. Here's what she said:

"We disliked the school board and they seemingly felt the same way about us. It was a lose-lose situation and I knew we were destined to walk the picket lines. At the last minute we accepted a contract offer and started school on time. The beginning of the year is stressful enough and this added pressure made it impossible to get excited about welcoming my students for yet another fun filled school year."

Here's what Andrea, a 20-year veteran experienced: "Three months into the school year I was called into the principal's office because several comments I made during a training seminar were taken out of context. Two things angered me: one of my colleagues ratted me out and the principal believed what he had been told and demanded I send an email to everyone in the session to clarify the comments I didn't make. With a heavy heart and angry scowl I did as instructed. From that moment on I felt like I was on the watch list—which was totally foreign to me. I prided myself on being a good teacher, staying above the fray and political issues that often permeate our profession, by doing a good job and keeping the students' best interest at heart.

In essence I did what was asked of me and a whole lot more. But it didn't seem to matter.

It seemed as though I was labeled a bad teacher—and that hurt."

Latisha, who's worked for two school districts during her 16 year career explains another difficulty teachers face: "Toward the end of the school year I received an insulting phone call filled with racial slurs and slanderous remarks from a student's parent. I thought I had a congenial relationship with this parent's child and felt violated, confused and angry when I hung up the phone. I had always been able to placate the most irate parent, but this was different. There was no communicating with this evil woman and it took every ounce of decorum to refrain from calling her—and her child—a few choice words. I didn't because I knew it would further cement her thoughts about me and my ability to teach my class."

Every year teachers are moved to different buildings within their school district for various reasons which causes anxiety and worry.

This stressful ordeal left one teacher strapped to a gurney and transported to the local hospital, and another running from the building in tears. It didn't matter if they had built a successful sports program for the past 20 years.

Johnny, a 20 year veteran summed it up perfectly: "The politics involved in this profession sometimes reminds me of a scene from a Sci-Fi movie where the villain gets to decide who lives and who dies."

Interviewing teachers and hearing all of these heartbreaking stories was taxing; I decided to come up with ways in which to help teachers feel calmer and more relaxed. I was able to deal with the stress, turmoil and crisis that I face on a daily basis because, unlike most of my colleagues I am a life coach.

What I learned from hearing all of these "year from hell" stories is that teaching is one of the most stressful occupations in the world, and most people don't know what to do to deal with the stress and turmoil at the end of the day.

It's this kind of stress that drives nearly half of all new teachers to other careers during the first five years of their career and causes countless others to seek medical advice for a wide range of maladies that stem from stress. The worst part is that nothing is being done.

For years I wanted to teach classes on stress management but couldn't find funding. No one seemed interested in the health and wellbeing of teachers, but I knew firsthand what was happening to me and my colleagues around the globe.

I'm grateful for all the year from hell stories because it finally made me do something.

Every year millions of brave men and women enter schools all around the world hoping to create change and share knowledge and assess their students' growth. They have no idea how to handle the barrage of negative emotions that result from stressful thoughts and immense deadlines. They are oblivious to how this stress affects every area of their lives. They know nothing about the ill-effects it has on their bodies, how it makes them crave sugary foods, how these foods add inches to their waistlines, and how this extra weight leads to a wide variety of illnesses that can seriously impact their quality of life.

It took me two years to write this book and during that time I was taught, firsthand, what it felt like to deal with the death of several students, get a horrible evaluation, face health problems, and have great friends moved to other buildings. It was as though the mighty Powers of the Universe wanted me to have an intimate knowledge of these subjects so I could share how I authentically coped with them. I'd much rather have interviewed someone who had experienced them but understanding each obstacle helped me fully know what it takes to overcome them.

My intention in writing this book is to share successful strategies to cope with all the stressors that many have accepted as a regular part of their work life.

Teaching is demanding, stressful and fraught with a million uncertainties in any given moment during the day. The stressors teachers face due to state and federally mandated testing and a flawed evaluation system affects them physically and mentally which in turn leads to autoimmune diseases and other health maladies. They teach in outdated buildings filled with mold and asbestos. School districts aren't able to remediate these issues because of budget restraints which are harming students and killing teachers. In the past 19 years 44 teachers around the world went to work with every expectation of going home at the end of the day but didn't because of gun violence. According to the U.S. Department of Education, from 2011-12, approximately:

➡ 20% of public school teachers reported being verbally abused.

➡ 10% reported being physically threatened.

➡ 5% reported being physically attacked in schools.

From 1997-2001, 1.3 million nonfatal crimes (including 473,000 violent crimes) were committed against America's teachers.

These are all real problems that need real solutions. It is my sincere intention to help teachers learn how to manage stress and get the help they need to live emotionally happy and fulfilling lives. We can't wait for our school districts and government officials to change the way schools are run. We get to make that change, internally, by ourselves, and by doing so we get to BE HAPPE.

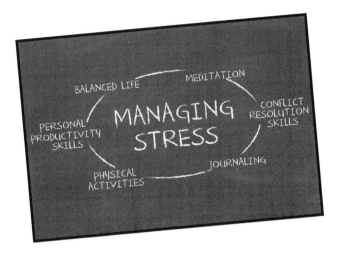

CHAPTER 1
NEGATIVE EFFECTS OF
CONSTANT STRESS

IN HIS BOOK, *The Teacher's Ultimate Stress Mastery Guide,* Jack Singer writes: "Our brains do not differentiate real dangers from those we craft in our minds when we worry about actual or anticipated disturbing events in our lives. Each psychological response to life-threatening stressors serves a critical, life-preserving purpose; but our bodies were designed only to activate this SNS (sympathetic nervous system) infrequently and when our lives are actually in danger, the daily switching on that so many of us experience because of our worrying puts tremendous strain on the system. The result is the potential physiological damage. Therefore, as scientists Robert Sapolsky (1998) and Hans Seyle (1976) describe, each adaptive response has a debilitating consequence for the human body when it is triggered frequently by worries and concerns:

➡ Blood continually leaving the GI tract to flow into the muscles of the legs and arms preparing for the fight, flight, or freeze reaction can lead to vomiting, energy loss, and chronic digestive problems, including gastritis and irritable bowel syndrome.

➡ People who are constantly under stress frequently have embarrassing perspiration issues, including dampness when shaking hands.

➡ Muscles continually tightening up can lead to muscle spasms, tension, and pain, particularly in the neck and back. In addition, chronic muscles tension contributes to migraine and tension headaches, jaw clenching, and fatigue.

➡ Glucose spilling into the bloodstream often contributes to diabetes and other endocrine disorders.

➡ The chronic worrier or anxious person triggers the brain to spill adrenalin continuously into the bloodstream. Because of a function of adrenalin is to keep you alert, a side effect of having too much adrenalin residing in your bloodstream is insomnia. This is why so many highly stressed people have sleeping difficulties.

➡ Although cortisol is necessary to prepare the muscles for vigorous reactions in the face of danger, the continual release of cortisol into the bloodstream blocks the removal of certain acids and breaks down lean tissue to convert to sugar for energy in the survival scenario. This causes ulcerations in the lining of the stomach, which is why so many people diagnosed with ulcers are people suffering from chronic stress. Long-term, chronic release of stress hormones like cortisol damages the body in many ways and leads to many diseases.

➡ Frequent blood clotting puts a person at a great risk for stroke or heart attack.

➡ Suppressing your immune functioning because of the constant switching on of the SNS can lead to distress consequences in terms of fighting infections and protecting you from immune system disorders, including allergies, arthritis, AIDS, lupus, some cancers, the common cold, and the flu.[8]

If you've been in the teaching profession long enough, you know firsthand the various illness colleagues have experienced or perhaps you have had one of the medical issues mentioned in this book.

It's essential to realize it's not just being around a classroom of germ-carrying students that makes you sick. It's your thoughts that do you in more than anything else.

"It's important to understand that the stressors we face are not actually provoked by the events that take place in our lives daily but how we interpret and think about those events—what we say to ourselves about those events. We can set off our emergency response by simply thinking about these events or anticipating potential problems befalling us in the future."[9]

The good news is that you don't have to live like that. You get to enjoy your life and your job. Heck, you even get to leave the profession or do other jobs within the organization if you so desire. It's only when you feel as though you're stuck and buying time until you're able to retire that you may begin to notice a wide range of illness. Life is too precious to live like that. You get to help students learn and grow and this can be an extremely rewarding job if you let it. It's in that spirit I've created a seven-step plan to help you combat the negativity and stress that seems to be the norm in our profession. The next seven chapters will spell out the BE HAPPE plan and give you concrete advice and examples on how you can live happier in every area of your life.

B = Be aware of the signs and symptoms of burnout

E = Eliminate emotional baggage

H = Healthy mind and body practices

A = Avoid unnecessary stress

P = Permission to follow your passion

P = Plan for another career

E = Enjoy every aspect of your life.

CHAPTER 2
FLORENCE'S STORY:

What teaching does to your body

FLORENCE MOYER WAS BORN TO TEACH: "From the time I can remember I wanted to be a teacher. I thought I would eventually get my PhD and teach college but life had other plans for me,"[1] she said.

She graduated in 1978, when there were more than enough teachers—which meant small salaries.

"I took a kind of a windy path. I got an undergrad degree in political science, which I loved, and then I went straight to business school because I love school and if you're going to be a teacher, you kind of love school. So

I had an MBA when I was 24, with the idea that I would get a PhD and teach college. I fell in love with college and thought of becoming a college professor. I did the business thing in my 20s and hated it. It was totally not a good fit for me and I had a quarter-life crisis. The year I turned 29 is when I quit my job and went back to music school because that's what I always loved doing."

Florence subbed for a couple of years and started her master's degree part-time. "I ended up teaching the first four years of my career in a small private girls high school—a catholic high school. I taught music there and I loved it. I absolutely loved it. I directed two choirs. I directed a couple of bell choirs. I taught music theory. I taught private boys lessons and it was really, really a lot of fun. I didn't make enough money to live on, but the church job helped and I really enjoyed the atmosphere. It was very collegial. The kids were motivated and were nice. They were fun."

After getting her master's degree Florence began working in a middle school.

"On the first day I watched my principal interact with a colleague. The principal was just so mean that I came home and cried so hard that night because I felt I had totally made the wrong decision. I felt I had to stay because school was starting and I don't have another job," she said. Florence taught fifth through eighth grade. "I loved teaching middle school and had a great time with them. I loved that in the beginning all of the faculty members had the same philosophy on what to teach. We had the same guidelines but we were able to be really creative around that," she said.

After the first six years she began to experience upper respiratory issues. "It got more and more stressful when I got sick around the middle of October and I started with a sinus infection. The conventional wisdom was, 'it's just a cold because you're not used to being around kids' and I discovered I was usually sicker at school and good when I was at home and halfway through the weekend I would feel better and then by Monday night I'd feel sicker."

After a year or two of investigating, Florence realized there was one classroom where something was not right in the air system that caused her and other teachers in her department to get sick. One teacher literally had to quit because she was having so many respiratory problems.

Although Florence enjoyed teaching the constant health issues made life difficult. "I got to the point where after five years I decided to do something about it because I didn't want to be sick the whole winter. I went to the principal and was told, 'there's no problem' because they had just done a remodel there and blah, blah, blah. They had a custodian sit in my classroom every day for a week with a thing that was supposed to measure the air quality. Of course they determined there was nothing wrong but I kept getting sick."

Things continued to worsen for Florence. "It all started to fall apart after my sixth year there. There were four music teachers in the building. There was a team of core teachers who had been there for a long time. There was some turnover but not a lot. The four of us worked really well together; we certainly had our struggles and disagreements but philosophically we were the same. At the end of the day we all wanted the same thing for the kids. We helped each other to make that happen. One retired and one got sent up to the high school. So the two of us remaining were excited about the year to come. We worked really, really well together and we overlapped our kids and had the same philosophy together and were so excited. We found out at the end of August the other teacher was being shipped down to one of the elementary schools and I was splitting time between two schools. Are you kidding me? That was just crazy! At that point I think I was third highest in terms of seniority of music faculty but they put me in two schools. They brought in three brand new teachers and told them not to listen to any of the old teachers: make something new and create it your way. There was this incredible shift in the schedule and political change where all of a sudden any loyalty, any seniority or any sense that I knew what I was doing, and the feeling that I was a good person to listen to for ideas was completely thrown out the window. So I was in two new schools with all new students and then it got totally worse. I was exhausted from the very beginning. It was an emotional shock and I had to work through that. Just being able to do that schedule and having to reconnect with the kids and traveling back and forth with no home base was horrific. I did that for a year and it was horrible."

After being moved back to her old school the next year and having to travel to two schools again the year after that, Florence had had enough. "The deal breakers were whatever was going on physically in the building that was making me sick and the constant change that felt like it was more than what was going on everywhere else. What I mean by that is that change is inevitable and it happens faster and faster and public education is going through earth-shattering changes but there were so many that it felt like it was just happening to me and not the people around me. And that's when I finally decided that I was at an age where if I was to make something of my coaching business it was time to quit."

Katie Daniel's Story

Katie Daniels had a problem similar to Florence's in that her symptoms started negatively affecting her health about three or four years into her teaching career. She remembers being perfectly fine during the summer.

"By the second day of school I would still feel okay but by the third day I'd be suffering from an asthma attack or sinus infection and it has happened in every school I've ever taught in."

She kept thinking she was the problem until she was hired at her fifth school where she's taught for the past 14 years. "I had no idea it was a chronic thing. Anytime we'd have an extended vacation I'd be fine and when I'd get back in school I'd be sick," she said. She finally figured out it had to be directly attributed to the school environment. After a recent school construction project Katie saw firsthand what was making her sick.

"My classroom was down the hall from the construction site and I saw mold, rodent feces, cockroaches, raccoons, and other rodent nests up in the ceilings. The construction guys were pretty grossed out. The nests had been there for years and I could hear them running inside the tin vents in my classroom. As soon as the weather started to get a little chilly they'd come into the nest and start scurrying in the vents."

Katie recalls how a couple of times they even pushed the ceiling tiles down onto the computers and the students' desks in her classroom.

This has taken a toll on Katie's health. "I get sinus infection, upper respiratory infections, bronchitis, pneumonia, ear infections, and anything related to respiratory issues," she said. That all changed when her school purchased an air purifier for her classroom. "I could physically feel the difference and haven't had to be hospitalized in a few years," she said. The good news is that Katie's administrators footed the bill for the air purifier to ensure she could continue to teach in her classroom.

The Doctor's Prognosis

Dr. Dennis Rademaker has treated teachers like Florence and Katie for the past 30 years. "I see this a lot in the teaching occupation especially because these are older buildings. I was watching television the other night and they were still using a building somewhere in Hammond, Indiana that's 85 years old. Most of these buildings are older and school districts don't have money to replace or improve the infrastructure. So you get aging ventilation systems and lack of filtration. Many of them have boilers where you can't filter the air out and, on top of that, a lot of them have flat roofs or structures that are prone to flooding and you get mold growth in there,"[2] explained Rademaker. The key difference is someone suffering from environmental allergies like Katie and Florence is that their symptoms disappear during long breaks from school. "I see this in a lot of teachers who are better when they're away from the environment and as soon as they go back they start to have problems again. I think it's inherent in that kind of occupation," he said.

Dr. Rademaker continued, "The other problem is that a patient with a mold allergy will have a reaction while another teacher who isn't allergic will be perfectly fine so administrators and maintenance people have trouble dealing with that because not everyone is affected. Mold allergies are an allergic response to the mold and it starts causing sinus congestion, ear problems, asthma and all of these things causes inflammation and swelling that leads to increased infection which can be a never-ending cycle."[2]

Treatment varies from patient to patient according to Dr. Rademaker.

"Some patients need anti-inflammatory sprays and preventative asthma medications. When they get sick they have to go on Prednisone and breathing treatments. In some cases we put patients on allergy shots to try to reverse their immune response. There are a whole host of medicines that are needed; Katie is not alone. I saw a teacher the other day who said the ceiling tiles in her classroom were getting wet and the remediation tends to be, 'let's put in a drop ceiling or let's throw carpeting on the floor' instead of putting in a new floor. Remediation often makes the problem worse. She said the tiles in her room were getting moldy and instead of going up and fixing the problem they just kept putting in new tiles. She said she would push up on the tiles and all this fine dust would come down. She's another one who was significantly affected when she was at work,"[2] he said.

Dr. Rademaker recommends the following for teachers who are suffering some of the same symptoms as Florence and Katie:

➡ Get tested to figure out if your classroom environment is causing a problem. If you test negative to mold, dust mites, and roaches then there could be something else going on.

➡ Once you get tested you can go through the environment and see, like Katie did, whether or not your school district will purchase or let you run an air purifier in your classroom which can at least help control that environment.

➡ Be proactive. Talk to your administrators about your health issues and get a doctor's note. Sometimes that's the only thing that will force them to make your work environment healthier for you.[2]

Environmental Toxins

Another issue with environmental toxins is that they can cause a variety of autoimmune diseases such as Lupus and Rheumatoid Arthritis.

A 2007 story published by the John Hopkins Arthritis Center reported that teachers are more likely to die from autoimmune disease such as Multiple Sclerosis, Rheumatoid Arthritis and Systemic Lupus Erythematosus (SLE) than the general population.[3]

Another study by University of Connecticut researchers revealed that over an 11-year period, the mortality rate from autoimmune diseases for K-12 teachers was twice the rate than those in other professional occupations. Even more surprising, the death rate from the diseases for high-school teachers was 12 percent higher than for elementary school teachers. Teachers could be exposed to the environmental factors that raise their risk of contracting an autoimmune disease early in their careers, according to the UConn study.[4]

"This was not released to be alarming," says Dr. Stephen J. Walsh, who prepared the study. "But it is clear that something is going on among schoolteachers; many of them have health problems. New groups of people enter the profession every year—people who become at-risk when they enter the classroom. Autoimmune diseases occur when the body's immune system attacks certain organs as if those organs were infecting agents. Many of the diseases—which include multiple sclerosis, systemic lupus, and rheumatoid arthritis—are diagnosed in people between the ages of 25 and 30; complications from the diseases often begin to cause death 10 to 15 years later. Other studies have suggested one possibility for the higher mortality rate among secondary teachers, Walsh says. It appears that the Epstein-Barr virus—the virus that causes mononucleosis, one of the few infectious diseases most common among the teen-age population—sets off some autoimmune illnesses."[4]

Both elementary and high school teachers also had a four percent higher mortality rate from rheumatic fever, another autoimmune disease, than did people in other professions; in the 35 to 44 age group, the number is elevated to 62 percent higher. Scientists know, however, that the trigger for rheumatic fever can be the streptococcus bacteria, which is also the cause of strep throat, a common ailment in children.[4]

In the article in Education World, The National Education Association (NEA) agrees that exposure to infections in poorly ventilated buildings could be a factor in teachers' rate of autoimmune diseases. "Above fifth grade, teachers are exposed to about 140 kids a day, Walsh said. "Over 20 years, that is a lot of people-exposure. Fifty percent of our teachers are in schools in need of repair. We have to start asking questions about air quality, paint, lead, and asbestos. There is a lot to know and a lot to find out."[4]

Asbestos.com, a for-profit advocacy group, researches the latest data about asbestos and asbestos-related diseases to ensure accurate, up-to-date information to help victims of asbestos exposure. They provided the following information:

Asbestos in schools

Ceiling tiles, vinyl floor covering and the duct work for the heating and cooling system all may contain asbestos.

Students and school employees face significant health risks from lingering asbestos in schools and colleges across the U.S. Because the current policy is to manage asbestos materials in-place, the potential for harmful exposures will likely persist for years to come.

One area of concern for parents and teachers is the prevalence of asbestos in U.S. school buildings. If a school was built before the 1980s, it's likely that it contains some form of asbestos. About half of all schools in the U.S. were built from 1950 to 1969, when asbestos materials were highly prevalent in construction.

When maintenance work disturbs these materials, or they start to deteriorate over time, asbestos dust can enter the air and be inhaled. Exposure to the dust puts teachers and students at increased risk for mesothelioma, lung cancer and other serious lung conditions.

Asbestos Cover-Up

According to the Environmental Protection Agency (EPA), asbestos-containing materials reside in many of the approximately 132,000 primary and secondary schools in the nation. These schools serve more than 55 million children, and are the worksites for more than 7 million teachers, administrators and support staff.

As long as asbestos building materials remain in good condition, the EPA insists they pose minimal health risks and recommends schools leave them in place. But if negligent maintenance work or improper abatement procedures occur, otherwise harmless asbestos products can cause serious exposures.

Health Risks for Teachers

While the occupations at highest risk for asbestos exposure have historically been miners, construction workers and veterans of the U.S. Armed Forces, teachers are more likely to be exposed than many other occupations that don't directly involve asbestos.

The elementary and secondary schools industry ranked second for mesothelioma deaths in 1999, according to National Center for Health Statistics (NCHS) data on reported causes of death. Construction topped the list with 77 deaths, and teachers followed with 38 deaths.

More teachers died of mesothelioma that year than workers in other industries known for frequent asbestos exposure risks, including industrial chemicals, railroads and electric light and power.

The problem is not just relegated to the U.S., it's worldwide. Media reports in England estimates that 75 percent of the 24,372 schools in England have buildings that contain asbestos-containing products. The National Union of Teachers refutes this number estimating the number closer to 86 percent. A story on BBC by Victoria Derbyshire reported that between 2003 and 2012, 224 teachers died of cancer.[5]

With diminishing budgets, school districts put building infrastructure issues on the back burner, which leads to increased teacher and student exposure that has proven to cause debilitating diseases after prolonged exposure. Another issue that is more threatening than the environment teachers work in is the damage stress does to the minds and bodies of teachers.

CHAPTER 3
NAMING THE STRESSORS

TEACHING IS REGULARLY LISTED as one of the most stressful jobs in the world. The fact that no two days are ever the same and the multitude of challenges of dealing with students, parents, administrators and colleagues presents a wide variety of stressors during the course of an average school day. There aren't many jobs where people average 60 hours per week for a little more than $18 an hour (based on a $50,000 salary).

Stress seems to be something teachers expect as part of their daily lives but many aren't aware of the toll it is taking on their bodies, minds, and family life. In her bestselling book Strive, Arianna Huffington writes, "Women in stressful jobs have a nearly 40 percent increased risk of heart disease, and a 60 percent greater risk of diabetes. In the past 30 years, as women have made substantial strides in the workplace, self-reported levels of stress have gone up 18 percent.[6] That makes perfect sense in that women's roles as the primary caretaker in the family have not changed although there are many households where this is not the case. It is therefore imperative that teachers understand the various forms of stress and how those impact their daily lives.

Dr. Robert Litchfield has practiced cardiology for the past 40 years. He explains there has been an increase in literature explaining how stress affects the heart in a negative way. "It turns out there are volumes of recent literature showing simple stress that is multiplied under time constraints can cause increased heart rate and blood pressure. These all result in increased catecholamine which are hormones produced by the adrenal glands. Catecholamine is released into the blood when a person is under physical or emotional stress. The main catecholamines are dopamine, norepinephrine, and epinephrine (which used to be called adrenalin). This acute or short-term stress is a result of too many demands and not enough time to fulfill them.[7] To a teacher, this sounds like an everyday occurrence.

Dealing with a difficult student first thing in the morning is a lot less stressful than dealing with a similar student at the end of the day. Any teacher who has had to deal with multiple difficult students during the course of a school year knows intimately what this kind of stress feels like. Too much short-term stress can lead to a wide variety of physical and mental ailments.

Acute Stress

Acute stress symptoms for teachers include stacks of ungraded papers, lesson planning, photo copying assignments, parent phone calls, doctors' appointments, grocery shopping, as well as all the other personal errands they need to run after school.

Acute stress is the least harmful because the little things teachers stress about are normally completed in a day or two and it is the easiest form of stress to manage and treat.

Episodic Acute Stress

You may be prone to suffer acute stress frequently if you're anything like I used to be.

Most mornings during the school year my alarm sounded around 5 a.m., and I was normally out the door by 6:30. My morning routine included packing lunches for my two kids and me because there was rarely enough time to grab lunch in the teachers' cafeteria because my nonstop schedule of teaching three different classes kept me constantly in motion. There were lessons to plan, papers to grade and never-ending yearbook deadlines that continuously threatened my sanity. To keep up I worked nights and weekends. At least once a month I would drive more than 60 miles roundtrip to the 24-hour post office to avoid missing a deadline. This nonstop cycle of never-ending deadlines caused lots of sleepless nights.

During my push to never miss a deadline I neglected my kids, gained at least 20 pounds from all the fast food I constantly consumed because I no longer had time to cook all while I pushed myself to sheer exhaustion. But the work had to be done—at any cost—and I paid dearly. I lived an unorganized and extremely chaotic life. I had no idea I was living with acute stress.

We've all experienced a coworker, boss or parent that has been short-tempered, irritable, anxious and tense; they're no fun to be around. They're like virtual Tasmanian devils with their constant stream of negative energy wreaking havoc wherever they go. They're always in a rush, quite rude and often hostile toward anyone who has the misfortune of crossing their paths. Working with them is like walking an invisible tightrope because you never know when you're going to be the victim of their anger or hostility. In every school there are normally a few teachers and administrators who fit this description and the simple reason is that they may be suffering from an acute form of stress.

Another form of stress comes from the professional worrier who constantly forecasts the worst-case scenario whenever given the chance. They're the teacher who hates kids that look a certain way, are from a certain part of town or the kid who is related to the student they hated five years ago. No matter what's happening in the world they tend to take the pessimistic outlook and love to share their oh-so-sad stories with you.

I once worked with Annie who worried about every single person in her family even though they were all doing fabulous things in the world. She also relished in being able to worry about me and my kids as well. Once I sheepishly shared that I planned to leave teaching someday and pursue life coaching fulltime. Every time she saw me for the next three years she'd nervously ask if I'd saved enough money and what would I do if I quit my job and had a health crisis or my kids needed to move back home or I didn't have enough money to live on. Her incessant need to worry about everyone drove her nuts— and everyone around her as well. After experiencing quite a few health problems she decided to quit. I'm sure that decision was agonizing for her and her family and I'm sure she's still worrying about money and her health and her kids' health and the stock market and global warming and anything else that enters her thoughts.

What all of these people have in common is the fact that their stress levels are constantly elevated over a long period of time. Dr. Litchfield explained what happens to the heart after prolonged stress, "Catecholamines (hormones made in the adrenal glands and formerly called adrenaline) increase with stress. An extreme example is when one is walking in Africa and is confronted by a tiger. In that situation one's heart rate and blood pressure increases and the pupils dilate. These are clear physical manifestations of stress."[7] The truth is that there are no tigers roaming in the halls of our schools but our bodies react as though there are.

It's difficult to understand these repetitive patterns when they've been a part of your belief system your whole life. It's like asking my worrywart friend to just stop worrying. She simply can't without first realizing it's a problem and then seeking some sort of professional help to change it. It might stem from her belief that her incessant hovering and anxiety actually keep everyone safe while everyone around her thinks the exact opposite. These kinds of habits and beliefs kept her stuck in a pattern of panic and despair. She blamed everyone and everything when her thoughts and actions simply were the culprits.

Chronic Stress

Chronic stress is the result of months or years of prolonged episodic stress. It is most harmful to your body—and every part of your life. People who suffer from this long-term stress normally hate their jobs (burnout), are dealing with an addiction, or may be dealing with a family problem (ending a marriage or experiencing a severe breakup).

Dr. Litchfield explains, "Patients under severe emotional stress can develop heart failure that is unrelated to coronary artery disease, hypertension, or any other medically diagnosed disease. Recently I had an elderly patient whose husband had passed away and was experiencing severe heart failure. The sole cause of her heart failure was broken heart syndrome also known as Takosubo cardiomyopathy. This cardiomyopathy manifests as a ballooning out of the anterior wall or the front of the heart much like a balloon tire on a car just before it ruptures as a blowout."[7]

I am sure this is what happened to the teacher who was carried out of school on a gurney after he found out he would be transferred to another school. The thought of leaving a school he had made his home for more than 25 years left him strapped to that gurney, and most likely, caused in him the same symptoms the elderly patient experienced after her husband passed away.

Prolonged exposure to stress effects can also elevate your blood pressure. Dr. Litchfield explains, "It is also well known that chronic high blood pressure creates a thickening of the heart muscle known as left ventricular hypertrophy. Longstanding high blood pressure leads to heart failure and dialysis." By lowering your stress hormones you can reduce your high blood pressure, which in turn reduces your chances of getting long-term heart disease. The inverse is also true according to Dr. Litchfield, "An unopposed high catecholamines state will result in end-stage heart disease."[7]

If you lead a hectic life, it can be normal to feel as though you're constantly running a never-ending marathon. For years I excused it away as just a part of the job when it wasn't. I had no idea how I was compromising my health by simply ignoring the symptoms I experienced. I felt like

I was a good teacher because I was constantly pushing myself to do more in less time when in reality that was the worst thing I possibly could have done to myself and my family. Florence Moyers knows all too well what it feels like to experience chronic stress. "I knew I was burned out and didn't feel like there was any help for me. We had an employee assistance program through our district and I was just trying to keep so many balls in the air and feeling so busy and feeling so overwhelmed; just the idea of taking the time to talk to anyone was overwhelming. So instead of seeking formal help I created places for that to happen on my own with singing and running,"[1] she said.

It took Florence a while before she began to change her life: "I did the 'walking wounded' thing for a long time. Being a music teacher the whole 'show must go on' kind of thing; I can't tell you how many times I went in sick because it was the day of the chorus rehearsal and I didn't really mind doing that. That was prime time for me. I loved being with the kids. I was miserable and it was horrible and I hated it."[1]

Florence shared she wishes she had found professional help instead of suffering in silence for so long. Most people think they can handle all of the pressures of the job. Some can while others can't.

CHAPTER 4
BE AWARE OF THE SIGNS AND
SYMPTOMS OF BURNOUT
Burnout: The silent epidemic

APPROXIMATELY HALF OF ALL NEW TEACHERS in the U.S. leave the profession within the first five years; the number is much higher in urban school districts. I was shocked to learn that teachers can begin to feel the symptoms of burnout as early as student teaching— until I remembered my student- teaching days. Research shows that of those who leave within five years burnout is cited as the main cause.

I always thought experienced teachers experienced burnout more than their younger, inexperienced colleagues but that is not the case according to a published research report by Dr. Molly Fisher of The University of Kentucky.[10] Student teachers may be more susceptible to burnout because of their lack of experience in dealing with the day-to-day demands of planning, teaching and implementing lessons. This is in addition to attending professional development meetings, contacting parents, the multitude of clerical tasks associated with teaching, contacting school personnel to get assistance for a special needs student and simply remembering to eat lunch and get in a bathroom break at least once during the hectic school day.

Dealing with other people's kids is hard—especially the difficult ones who hate school and everything associated with it. We enter the classroom with the mindset that everyone will learn and sit quietly and do as they are told. Sadly this doesn't happen all the time, which causes great angst, frustration and stress. Too much angst, frustration and stress leads to burnout. It makes you feel as though what you do and how you do it just isn't right. You may even tend to think there's something wrong with you when, in fact, it's simply one of the stresses of the job. It leaves you feeling drained and exhausted without any warning that you're experiencing the symptoms of someone who is burned out.

I personally think this can be a good thing.

It reminds me of a story by Oprah Winfrey: "I say the universe speaks to us, always, first in whispers. And a whisper in your life usually feels like 'hmm, that's odd.' Or, 'hmm, that doesn't make any sense.' Or, 'hmm, is that right?' It's that subtle. And if you don't pay attention to the whisper, it gets louder and louder and louder. I say it's like getting thumped upside the head. If you don't pay attention to that, it's like getting a brick upside your head. If you don't pay attention to that—the brick wall falls down. That is the pattern that I see in my life and so many other people's lives. And so, I ask people, 'What are the whispers? What's whispering to you now?"[11]

Burnout is kind of like that. There are a series of disregarded incidents that lead to a slow burn. Sometimes it seemingly comes out of the blue. One minute you're enjoying your teaching career then something happens to change it all. If you're anything like me, you remember the exact moment it happened.

It was a regular school day. I received an email from an administrator asking me to come into the office to talk about a problem I was having with a teacher with whom I shared a classroom. After explaining yet another time what I had so eloquently written in an email, I was told in a very stern voice that I didn't own anything in that classroom. I didn't own the computers, the fancy dongles that made the video editing equipment work and I didn't get to tell another teacher what his students could and could not touch in the classroom that I did not own because I didn't buy the equipment. I didn't buy the desks. I didn't buy anything in that room so I couldn't decide who could and could not use the equipment. When I tried to explain that it was very expensive and very fragile, I was once again reminded in a stern tone that implied I was to shut the hell up and listen because he wasn't going to repeat that message again. I wasn't in charge. He was. He decided. I didn't, and it was in my best interest to do as I was told.

When I asked if he would be the one to replace the broken equipment he pointed toward the door and asked me to leave.

I was devastated and heartbroken and felt like I had just been spanked by my momma for calling someone a dirty name when all I tried to do was protect my costly equipment.

At that moment the flicker turned to a flame.

I didn't care anymore.

I didn't try.

I just did my job or the bare minimum of what I needed to do to keep from being fired.

The fun-loving, energetic, let's-think-of-something-new-to-do was gone and my students questioned where she had gone. I feigned ignorance and tried to resurrect the passion I once felt but it was too late. I had let them get to me.

They won, and all of my students lost.

They lost an energetic teacher who now did as little as possible to teach the lesson. It hurt like hell. I wanted to do more. I wanted to give my all like I used to but I couldn't.

I thought about quitting but didn't because I was too vested in the system. I was a single parent with one kid in high school and another in college. There was no way out so I faked the funk day after day as my love affair with my job burned the hell up until I got to the point where I was just going through the motions.

If you've ever loathed a job, you know what I mean. You do the bare minimum to get by. You teach what you've always taught. You long for Christmas and summer break. You wait until the last minute to plan lessons and most of the planning is actually done on the fly.

Then you feel guilty and try to do better but you can't.

You can't because you're experiencing a silent disease that no wants to talk about because you fear ridicule. The thought of losing your job keeps you quiet. Those suffering from this malady often blame themselves and not their jobs or their demanding bosses or never-ending deadlines. It's like a battered wife blaming herself for being battered. It just isn't true. Burnout is a simple math equation. You put in more time, energy and effort with little-to-no reward, satisfaction or enthusiasm. Your ability to juggle all of the demands of the job are next to impossible because you're running on an empty tank.

Some teachers may seek therapy to understand their inadequacy (like Florence wished she had done) while others look to anesthetize the problem with alcohol, drugs or other addictions that lessen the pain of going to a job they hate every single day. One of the first steps in combating burnout is acknowledging the debilitating stress that keeps you stuck in a never-ending cycle of fear, frustration, blame and shame. It's not your fault, but in order to get to the other side you first have to acknowledge the problem and then seek help.

Understanding that burning out is something that happens to most people in high-contact careers like teaching helped me tremendously. Knowing that I did the best I could in a difficult and damn-near-impossible situation helps the guilt I've carried the past few years. I decided to enter this profession later in life. I was 38 my first year of teaching and knew I could handle any pressures the job would bring. My faulty reasoning was based on the fact that I had survived six years of substitute teaching. In my own mind I was a seasoned veteran the first day I began teaching fulltime.

I had no idea I had entered a career where everyone experiences some degree of burnout during the course of his or her career. Some burnout really does begin during student teaching. Sometimes it takes a few years to start the slow burn that eventually worsens if left unmanned.

It's inevitable when you have constant contact with the same group of people for 180 days (an average school year) or more. It makes perfect sense that you would begin to question your ability to do your job at the same level and with the same intensity you once did because it's impossible to maintain the same level of enthusiasm and dedication you may have had during the early years of your career.

The sad part is that I knew none of this when I started teaching. I didn't learn it in any of my education classes and it was never a topic in any of the professional development meetings I've attended the past 17 years.

It's like this dirty little secret doesn't really exist and teachers are left to deal with a disorder that leaves them blaming themselves when, in fact, it's an inevitable part of the profession.

The most recognized burnout test was created by Dr. Christina Maslach, Professor of Psychology at the University of California at Berkeley. The Maslach Burnout Inventory can be accessed via the Web[12] for $15. In a New York Times article Dr. Maslach[13] explained the test asks questions in the following areas:

➡ Emotional exhaustion can result in being emotionally overextended, drained and used up without any source of replenishment. It's the chronic feeling that you just can't face another day.

➡ Cynicism or depersonalization means a loss of idealism. Particularly in the health professions, it can manifest itself as having a negative, callous or excessively detached response to other people.

➡ Reduced personal efficacy signals a decline in feelings of competence and productivity at work.

"While most people think job burnout is just a matter of working too hard, that's not necessarily true. Professor Maslach and Professor Leiter list six areas that can result in burnout: work overload; lack of control over the work; insufficient rewards; workplace community problems, such as incivility and a lack of support among co-workers; a lack of fairness, such as inequality of pay, promotions or workload; and a conflict between one's personal values and the requirements of a job."[13] But burnout isn't always a bad thing.

The Blessing of Burnout

Burnout can be a gift that allows you to pay attention and choose a different path. In her book, *The Joy of Burnout*, Dr. Dina Glouberman writes, "I am in the rather unusual position of arguing that although there is a great deal wrong with our society, our work-places, our relationships and our lives, burnout is ultimately positive if we are open to its message. This is because it asks us to become more of who we really are."[14]

I wholeheartedly agree.

When I was crashing and burning I did a lot of soul-searching and realized that I would not be able to continue to teach for the next 20 years. Every year seemed harder than the last and I had no idea how to walk away from a job that was my only source of income. It wasn't until I was faced with the prospect of getting a "Needs Improvement" rating on my biennial evaluation that I began investigating my exit strategy and submitted my retirement letter.

When I first began researching burnout I learned that teachers who overextend themselves by doing after-school activities like coaching and detention are more susceptible to burnout than their counterparts who go home at the end of the school day. It made perfect sense so I made some changes:

I traveled instead of teaching summer school.

I started exercising at least three days a week and gave up my after-school tutoring job.

I started writing and quilting.

In fact, burnout helped me in more ways than it hurt me. It helped me see that my teaching career was coming to an end and I should start making plans to do more of what I loved and less of what I didn't. It helped start the transitioning process from one career to another—just as it can for you. I've seen far too many coworkers struggle with this devastating disorder during the past 20 years and I'm hopeful they will now find the courage to face the fear and get the professional help they need to move toward a happier place in life because life is too short to do work that makes you mentally and physically ill.

I think the main reason I didn't listen to that small voice of knowing for so long is because I was too busy doing the whole "living a miserable life" kind of thing. I was newly divorced and desperately trying to figure out how to maintain the same standard of living on half the income. I was sad and scared to death of failing my kids while secretly wondering if I had just made the biggest mistake of my life. The best part is that small voice would send me signals that I was on the right path every now and then.

I would life-coach clients who desperately cling to their "shoulds" as though their life depended on it. They thought they should stay another six years in a job they desperately hated because of the pension. I've heard more than one disgruntle colleague say, "I'm not leaving any money on the table. I've earned my whole retirement and I'm going to collect it," to which I respond: Is your life worth it? Is knowing you may not live to fully enjoy all of the money you're so desperate to collect worth the gamble? I don't think so. I'm currently planning to retire early because the thought of working more than that makes me physically ill and to do so is against everything I know to be true.

When I listened to that voice and did as instructed, I found joy. I started my life-coaching business. I found a web designer and created a website. I wrote weekly blogs. I wrote a book and learned that the greatest gift I could ever give my kids and myself was the daily act of self-love. I designed presentations for our teacher fair and they were the first to fill up. This all led me to believe I was continually making the right choices. All of these things helped me understand who I was and ultimately tap into my original medicine which you'll read more about in chapter eight.

All along I kept getting the message that I was meant to do something bigger and help more people than 150 students who trek through my classroom each year.

Slowly but surely I found joy and defeated burnout. I now know that when I refused to listen to do the things that made me happy I was rewarded with the gift of burning the heck out. I use "rewarded" because in hindsight it was truly a gift that helped me see how far left I'd gone from the teacher who loved what she did to the miserable shell of a woman who tried with all her might to do the same kind of job with one-tenth the motivation. Since I didn't give up I found my calling and am now able to help others through what I overcame. One of the best things about recognizing you're burned out (or slowly burning out) is that you get to make a choice to move toward what makes you happy or stay stuck in a life filled with fear and anxiety. It all starts with you and how you want to live the rest of your life.

Florence gives the following advice: "One thing is to make sure what's going on outside school is the best that you can possibly make it. I sang in two community groups and those really kept me going. I started running for a while and the running really helped. Everything lined up when I made the decision to leave. It became clear that 2012 was the year for me to go. I bought a house and was saving money. I saw the writing on the wall that I was never going to go back. It was just going to become less about teaching and more about being the babysitter and more contention. The contract expired and I was at the point where I had started to build my business and had socked away a lot of money so I felt like I had the cushion. The barometer I used was when my monthly pension take-home pay was the same as my mortgage; I knew I was going to be okay. That all kind of converged in 2012. We had to turn in our retirement letter by mid-March so I turned it in on Leap Day. It felt so good. I thought it was cool. Everything became clear. In the beginning I blamed myself. I cleaned up my own mess and realized that I was good and got clear about what I valued and what was going on around me and it was never going to be the right fit and that's when I started laying the groundwork to make the move. The other thing that made it really, really hard was that I loved what I was doing. I was able to see a student with autism who could barely hold a guitar play a song at the end of the marking period."[1]

The Teacher's Support Network, an England-based nonprofit service estimates that 88 percent of their teachers experienced stress, 72 percent had anxiety, while 45 percent reported experiencing depression in the 2014 Education Staff Health survey report.[15] In the U.S. "teacher satisfaction has declined to its lowest point in 25 years from 44 percent to 39 percent being very satisfied. This marks a continuation of a substantial decline. Teacher satisfaction has now dropped 23 percentage points since 2008," according to the 2013 MetLife Survey of The American Teacher. [16]

The MetLife survey also reports: "Stress among teachers has increased since 1985. In 1985—the last time this question was asked and when job satisfaction was also low—more than one-third (36 percent) of teachers said they felt under great stress at least several days a week. Today, that number has increased; half (51 percent) of teachers feel under great stress at least several days a week. Elementary school teachers experience stress more frequently. They are more likely than middle-school or high-school teachers to say they feel under great stress at least several days a week (59 percent versus 44 percent versus 42 percent). The increase since 1985 in the number of elementary school teachers who experience great stress at least several days a week is also noteworthy—59 percent today compared to 35 percent in 1985."[16]

Some of the biggest stressors include increased workload, large class sizes, lack of parental involvement, classroom disruptions, lack of support by administrators, lack of funding for classroom supplies, implementing common core standards and standardized teaching that affects teacher evaluations, merit pay and school shootings.

Negative Ways Teachers Cope with Stress

Some cope by eating, drinking or using illegal drugs to stop the never-ending stream of to-do lists and feelings of inadequacy, depression and other ailments caused by too much stress.

If you teach long enough, you'll run into a colleague or two who's an alcoholic.

I remember one such fellow who reeked of alcohol as I passed him in the school library one morning. Since I considered him a friend, I pulled him aside and shared with him what I smelled. He apologized and explained that he had partied a little too much the night before and barely had enough time to brush his teeth before coming to work. He then begrudgingly admitted to wearing the same clothes he wore the previous day because the thought of looking for clean clothes was too much to handle in his current state.

Then there was another colleague who often sported glassy eyes and a reddish Rudolph-like nose. He too often smelled of alcohol year after year after year … until he retired. You see, it's easy for me to spot an alcoholic; I lived with one for most of my life and often joked that I was a human alcoholic detector.

Growing up with an alcoholic parent was heartbreaking and extremely difficult at times; working with one is no walk in the park either. It's amazing the amount of alcohol that is consumed when teachers get together. I often marvel that no one was ever arrested for drunk driving when they could barely walk after too many drinks. I'm not judging, just grateful that my predisposition to alcoholism has kept me from indulging in more than a Shirley Temple or glass of white wine.

A *New York Times* editorial dated January 21, 2009, titled, "Pencils down, Bottoms up,"[17] perfectly explains one aspect of why teachers drink.

"How and why teachers drink is a topic that rarely receives the discussion it deserves. For the average drinker, alcohol provides mental escape, but for teachers that escape is physical, too—after spending entire days surrounded by children or teenagers, we are retreating to the one place that will be—ideally—certifiably childfree. During school hours, nothing is more important than quadratic equations and auxiliary verbs, and nothing will ever be. The classroom is the bully pulpit from which we articulate an ironclad triumvirate of maturity—attention, organization, responsibility—that the real world renders pretty much unrealistic. In the bar, we finally loosen our ties, and life's beautiful imperfections return.[17]

People turn to drugs and alcohol for a variety of reasons to lessen the pain of an extremely stressful day, week or month. It becomes a problem when you get to the point that you rely on any substance to make you feel better.

I remember a coworker who kept an assortment of pills in a plastic sandwich bag. She once joked that she should separate them so she would know which pill did what. After thinking about it for a few seconds, she shrugged and said it didn't really matter because they all made her feel better.

The truth is that we all want to feel better and turning to drugs and alcohol just creates yet another problem to overcome.

Helpful Ways to Eliminate Burnout

Burnout is filled with dread and fear. It's heavy and uncaring. It takes twice as long to do a task. It's filled with shame, regret and lots of, "I wish I could put more energy into this _____," but you can't because the part of you that used to love or mildly like what you do is gone and the only way to get it back is to realize it's gone and then do the work to either get it back or find a new career.

The first step is admitting you're on the burnout spectrum, meaning you're somewhere between one and 10. One means you're just starting to burn out and 10 means you're a forest fire burning out of control. When I realized I was burned out I was at a seven on the burnout scale. I came to work regularly, explained what we were doing that day and then sat at my desk while the students did the worksheet or watched the film clip or worked on a project. There wasn't a lot of direct instruction because I couldn't muster enough energy to plan a lesson that would necessitate that much energy because I just didn't have it. When more than three students asked the same question I would do enough direct instruction to answer the question but that was it. To further clarify this for yourself, answer the questions in **Appendix A** under the title Elminate Burnout.

Take a good look at your answers to determine if you feel more positive or more negative when you read your answers. If you rated negative 1-5, you may be in the early stages of burnout. If you're six or above, you're experiencing significant signs and symptoms of burnout.

Once you know where you are on the burnout scale, you get to do two things. First, you get to determine if you need some sort of professional help from a therapist or life coach to get to a happier place. Then, it's important to understand that burnout happens to most people who are in high-contact fields like teaching, medicine, and police work. No matter what stage of burnout you're currently experiencing you'll find lots of tips to help extinguish the flame in the following chapters. It's also important to understand that blaming yourself or your environment only exacerbates the problem. You get to find peace and solace in your work life and that only comes with accepting your current state and doing the work to change it.

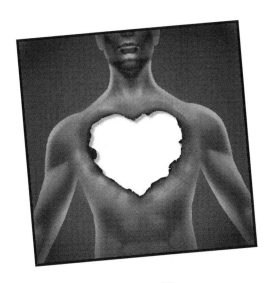

CHAPTER 5
ELIMINATE EMOTIONAL BAGGAGE
Dealing with students you love to hate

WES WAS A GREGARIOUS KID. He had long, flowing blond tresses during a time when they weren't really in style but he wore them well. He had a small frame and did almost anything he could to outrun the long shadow set by his older brother, who most teachers adored.

We got along fine the first few weeks of school and then I started seeing his defiant streak.

I did all the normal things: one-on-one talks about his behavior, phoned home, issued referrals, but nothing seemed to work.

My Television Production class was one of my busiest classes. It seemed as though there was never enough time to cover the content and I tried to utilize every minute of instruction. One of my classroom rules was that every student had to be inside the classroom and in their seat so that class could start immediately after the bell rang.

Wes would stand in the door with his big toe just over the threshold grinning from ear to ear with a mischievous look on his face when the bell sounded every single day, which made me want to yank his long flowy tresses into the classroom and drag him to his seat. I couldn't and he knew it. So he continued his shenanigans to get a rise out of me and laughter from his classmates. I had no idea how to tame his defiant streak. Major classroom disruptions weren't normally a problem for me. I'd nip them in the bud in just a matter of seconds but Wes' acts of daily defiance left me baffled.

I didn't figure out a way to fix the Wes Problem until I began planning a teacher workshop entitled "Creating a positive classroom environment." The irony was that Wes controlled my class. His deviously defiant behaviors undermined my lessons and I felt helpless and unable to control his behaviors.

Find Commonalities

During our first workshop session I had every teacher think of three of their least favorite students and then write all the reasons they disliked them, explain their defiant behaviors as well as what really pushed their buttons about their behaviors on one side of a large sheet of paper.

Then I had them list all the ways in which they were similar to their problem students. They had to explain how they exhibited the same behaviors as their little charges.

When I did this activity I learned Wes and I had a lot in common.

➡ We both had an older sibling that teachers adored.

➡ We both used inappropriate language at times.

➡ We both were defiant when we thought an injustice had been done.

➡ We both hated sitting though boring classes (in his case) and meetings (in mine).

➡ We both loved making people laugh.

➡ We both wanted people to like us.

Once I saw all the commonalities, I was able to soften a little and dislike him a little less. I also was able to get to know the real kid who constantly lived in his brother's shadow.

The teachers were instructed to strike up a random conversation with at least one student on their Do Not Like list at least a couple of times before our next session.

This meant I had to do the same with Wes. I had a real heart-to-heart with him one day after class and apologized for inadvertently comparing him to his brother all the time. I asked him why he took my Television Production class and he said he loved making movies and wanted to learn more about it. He also said his brother said I was a really cool teacher. Wes didn't agree. I laughed and shared how his foot just over the threshold made my blood boil every single day. He said that's why he did it. Once he knew a teacher's weak spot he took every liberty of using it. He knew just how far to take it and when to ease off.

He knew how to work the system and infuriate the hell out of me.

That day we made a truce.

He would stop his beginning-of-class shenanigans and I would let him be my special helper when I was teaching certain hands-on activities.

He agreed. We shook hands and our relationship changed—which made my life a whole lot easier. Years later Wes said that he wanted to know my breaking point. When I asked what he meant by that he explained that every teacher has a point where they just lose it. He said he just wanted to see my reaction when I got to that point, and when I didn't, he had to keep raising the stakes to push me there. I fully understood his point and it reminded me of another student who tried everything to get me to break and finally achieved it when he farted in my face as I sat on stool. I instinctively whacked him on his legs a few good times with a meter stick before realizing I most likely left welts on his legs. I was terrified and angry and insulted that a student would do such a thing in front of the whole class. He was immediately removed by security and I called his mom after class. Luckily she agreed I did the right thing and said she would be sure to deal with him when he got home. She apologized profusely and shared how embarrassed she was by his actions. I was happy she wasn't upset that a teacher had struck her little darling with a meter stick.

When I asked George why he had done this he said I was such a nice teacher and he often wondered what my breaking point was. One day he thought of the idea of farting in my face so he did and found out.

Managing a classroom full of students can be one of the most difficult parts of teaching. What I've found is that when I don't enforce classroom rules, I have an unruly class. When I do, the opposite is true.

Such was the case with both Wes and George. I failed to get across the message that such behaviors were unacceptable—even though I had no idea I needed to clearly state that farting in the teacher's face was not something one should never do. Now I clearly know better.

Every teacher I've ever had the pleasure of working with shows up every day with the intention of doing a good job, and discipline is an active part of what they do. It is something that needs to be done every single day for the rest of their teaching careers. I remember I used to think that once I covered the rules in the syllabus on the first day of school I had done my part. All I needed to say was "refer to your syllabus" and the students would magically stop doing what they were told not to do. Of course this doesn't work in the real world where it's all about constantly reinforcing the rules before things get out of control and knowing how to react and what to do when they do.

Trauma Kids: Teaching Students with a Big Hole in Their Hearts

Wouldn't it be great if students came with warning labels that clearly delineated their personal issues, family struggles, traumatic events, as well as their learning struggles and deficiencies? Then all we'd have to do was scan their labels to know their exact placement in our class along with which topics were difficult for them to deal with.

But life doesn't always work like that and we're left to figure this out on our own. A 2009 report entitle "Heling Children Learn" explains, "Children exposed to violence at home are often subject to the arbitrary will of caregivers who have unrealistic expectations for childhood behavior. Afraid to disappoint these caregivers and incur their explosive response, children often try, and inevitably fail, to meet these expectations. In their genuine desire for approval and success, these children may become perfectionists."[18]

Cindy was your average run-of-the-mill student. Her model looks, perfectly coiffed blond hair and stylish wardrobe made her one of the most popular girls in the school. She completed her assignments efficiently and begged for any homework in hopes of completing it before class ended. I admired her work ethic but not her rude and demeaning comments to her classmates and teacher. After several conversations, calls home and a few discipline referrals she told me that calling home was just a waste of time. I thought she was being defiant yet again, but something was different. I didn't get her "I don't give a damn what you do to me" stare she normally gave that would send shivers down the spine of a less-experienced teacher.

On this day I asked her why and she looked away and mumbled that her mom never answered the phone during the day. When I asked if she worked nights, she said no. She then blurted out that she was the one who worked most nights and she hated her job and wished she could just quit and join the cheerleading squad but she couldn't because she had to pay for all of her school expenses.

I later found out that her mom was an alcoholic and spent most of her days sleeping off nights of drinking. Cindy shared this information with me after I pulled her in the hall to explain that she'd have a tough time in college if she talked to her professors the same way she talked to me and her other classmates. She gave a halfhearted apology then began explaining how she felt pressured to be perfect and beautiful all the time and that she had to work so hard for everything she ever had. She wiped away tears as she explained that she hated how her life has changed since her parents divorced two years ago. Now she has to sit in a stupid class with stupid students who don't want to learn and all she *wants* to do was graduate and get the hell away from her mom who thinks drinking will solve her problems.

What I now know is that Cindy was unable to trust her classmates or me. "When children witness violence between their adult caregivers or experience abuse or neglect, they can enter the classroom believing that the world is an unpredictable and threatening place. Hopelessness, self-blame, and lack of control are typical of the feelings that can result from trauma; these feelings may lead to overwhelming despair and a loss of the ability to imagine the future or hope that circumstances will change. Children in this condition can be ill-prepared for the academic and social challenges of the classroom."[19]

Then there was Debby who witnessed her brother's killing by the neighborhood bully who had pushed her off the swing set a few minutes earlier. She ran home to tell her mom how the boy's shove made her fall and hurt both her knees. She said her brother grabbed her hand and they ran back to the park. After a few choice exchanges the bully pulled out a gun and shot her brother in the head. She said she didn't talk for four years and still blames herself for her brother's death. The report further explains, "Traumatized children often experience fear, anxiety, irritability, helplessness, anger, shame, depression, and guilt, but their ability to identify and express these feelings is often underdeveloped and poorly regulated. Some of these children may express emotions without restraint and seem impulsive, under controlled, unable to reflect, edgy, oversensitive, or aggressive. They may overreact to perceived provocation in the classroom and on the playground. Other traumatized children block out painful or uncomfortable emotions; they may appear disinterested, disconnected, or aloof. For them, the consequence of not knowing how to communicate or interpret emotions is the dampening or constricting of their feelings. Another group of traumatized children protect themselves from unmanageable stress and anxiety by dissociating—that is, by completely disconnecting emotions from the events with which they are associated."[20]

Steve hated school and his grades proved it. His spotty attendance didn't help either. When asked why he missed so much school he said, "Why come to a place where everybody hates you and makes you feel like you're stupid? I get enough of that at home." I didn't know this was a natural response for kids who experienced trauma at home. "Children who enter the classroom in a state of low-level fear may refuse to respond to teachers either by trying to take control of their situation through actively defiant behavior or, more passively and perhaps less consciously, by "freezing." Either way, the child is not receptive or responsive to the teacher or the demands of the classroom. Children who actively try to take control may be more overt and deliberate in their unwillingness to cooperate. This can be particularly frustrating for teachers since these children can appear to be in control of their behavior. Teachers often attempt to gain the compliance of "frozen" children via directives, but this approach tends to escalate the anxiety and solidify the inability to comply."[21]

Then there's Stella, who asked for a pass to the nurse. A few minutes later she returned saying that the nurse's office was closed. I quietly explained the assignment as she walked back to her seat. A few minutes later I heard a strange sound coming from the back of the classroom. When I asked Stella if she was okay she started crying uncontrollably while trying to explain that her ex-boyfriend was killed last night as he sat in a car outside his house. The whole class stared at her in shock as she tried to explain how she wanted to stay home but her mom made her come to school. Her painful cries made me well-up. My co-teacher (luckily there was another adult in the room) escorted her to the counselor's office and she went home. A few days later she returned and I never again saw the carefree gregarious girl that used to sit in my class.

What they all have in common is childhood trauma. It's estimated that one in four children in the U.S. witness a violent act and one in 10 children see a family member assault another person according to the federal National Survey of Children's Exposure to Violence, sponsored by the Office of Juvenile Justice Prevention and Delinquency Prevention and the Centers for Disease Control.[22]

I never heard of such a phrase until I started researching this book. I thought I'd write about difficult kids and how to calm their angst, not knowing that childhood trauma is a worldwide epidemic that affects millions of children every single school day. They come to school seeking a safe haven from the violence in their homes and communities and we, as a school community, fail them because we don't know they exist or even how to deal with them.

"The link between childhood trauma and trouble at school is strong, according to a 2011 study of 701 children from the Bayview Child Health Center in San Francisco. In that study, pediatrician Dr. Nadine Burke Harris found that a child with four or more adverse childhood experiences was 32 times more likely to be labeled with a learning or behavior problem than a child with no adverse childhood experiences. The categories of adversity include having a household member who is chronically depressed; having an incarcerated household member; living in a household with one or no parents; and living in a household with an alcohol and/or drug abuser."[23]

Please refer to **Appendix B** for additional information on how to teach students who have experienced childhood trauma.

After coming across this information I was able to pinpoint at least 10 students I recently taught that showed a few signs of being a traumatized student and going forward I feel as though I'm able to deal with them and create a supportive environment for them to learn. I never would have learned this information if I hadn't been researching ways in which to build stronger connections and relationships with my students and feel strongly that every school district should train their staff members to recognize and deal with the students who are walking around with huge holes in their hearts.

Plan for Distractions

Classroom management involves thinking about what possible problems there might be before they happen. After the first few days of school, you know who the distractors are. They'll ask personal questions in the middle of a lesson to get you off task. They'll throw something at another student just as you're giving a homework assignment or trying to explain a lesson. They're the kids you wish would magically disappear, but they don't.

While planning a recent lesson that involved using bundles of three highlighters that were secured together with a rubber band, I knew certain students would have problems with the rubber band so when I handed out the bundles, I took off the rubber band and put it on my wrist. When they asked why I did that, I told them I just wanted to make sure I had enough rubber bands. They looked at me kind of like my little dog Tommy does when I talk to him. He moves his head from side to side trying to process exactly what I'm saying. They tilted their heads too and I just kept passing out the highlighters. I didn't want to explain that I knew they would use them as weapons and shoot them across the room and most likely pay more attention to the little piece of rubber than the lesson I was teaching.

I just passed them out and avoided potential problems.

The bottom line in classroom management is being fair and respectful; it's extremely difficult. It would have been easy for me to berate and belittle Wes for his intentional disruptions in my class but that would have demoralized him and made me look like a moron. I think first and foremost our job is to teach students how to treat each other and we model that by how we treat them.

It's easy to allow your emotions to get the best of you. I've said things I wish I could take back; some I've caught and immediately apologized for in front of the whole class, but some I didn't catch.

Every year in each of my classes there are one or two students I do not like. I know admitting this may be akin to professional suicide, but it's the truth and my goal is to tell it like it really is. It's normally because they have severe behavior problems and I really don't want to deal with them. But since I can't click my ruby slippers three times and make them disappear, I get to teach them—lucky me.

What I've learned is these kids are disruptive for a reason and it's my job to use my detective skills to figure out why they behave in an inappropriate manner in my class and what I need to do to help them.

A few years ago I taught Kelly, who loved to talk to her friend so I purposely sat her on the other side of the classroom. When I asked her why she constantly yelled across the room she said, "I need to make sure she can hear me because you moved her too far away." She was right. I moved her because I thought that would solve her incessant talking. She decided to talk anyway.

Thus began my search to find out what made her tick. I discovered she was in the wrong class. Her reading and comprehension skills were too low for her to grasp the skills I was teaching, which explained her incessant distractions that detracted from her incompetence.

The solution in this situation was simple. She was tested and eventually placed in an appropriate class.

But what about the kids who are properly placed or are unable to be moved to another class?

For these kids you get to do a little work on yourself. It's about taking the time to look within and figure out what the story is you're telling yourself about this kid that's keeping you from building a healthy and productive relationship with him or her.

About 10 years ago I read *Loving What Is*, by Byron Katie.[29] It changed my perspective on people I don't like. It helped me to see that the only person I can change is me. I know it sounds a little Pollyannaish, but it works. In it Katie explains her process of doing "The Work" by questioning thoughts that make you feel some kind of emotional pain or suffering. I love this exercise so much that I have the app on both my iPhone and iPad.

Here's how it works:

Let's take my real-life student Elliott who refuses to do any work yet promises he's working on it or just finished it last night and forgot it at home. He also loves to throw things at a few of his friends who happen to sit on the other side of the room. I've had repeated talks with him and his mom and his dean about his behavior and lack of motivation in my class. What upsets me the most is his constant desire to use his cell phone during class. I've tried to reason with him, taken the phone and written several referrals but nothing seems to help. That is until I did *The Work.*

After doing the exercise I realized I treat him differently because I expect him to misbehave and play with his phone during class. I also expect him to fail so I'm not as kind and patient with him as I might be with another student. I also realized that he does his work some of the time, and in my mind he never does it. This caused me to doubt my ability to teach when in fact he was doing his work at least 60 percent of the time.

When you subconsciously harbor these kinds of stories, you are essentially causing additional stress and forcing yourself to negate all the good that you do. It's getting in touch with that part of you that knows the answers yet doesn't know how to access them.

This exercise saves me every single time I have a bad day at work. If I have a disturbing call with a parent I do The Work on it. If I feel as though I'm not doing enough to help a student or colleague or contributing more to the school community, I do The Work on it and it saves me from telling lots of stories that aren't true about me or my motivation to be a good teacher or a good mom or a good sister or a good friend. It also keeps my blood pressure in a healthy range and those pesky catecholamines from invading my blood stream.

The good news is that they are your thoughts and you

get to change them if you want. My favorite Byron Katie quote sums it all up very well: "When I argue with reality, I lose—but only 100 percent of the time."

End the Blame and Shame Game

There are times when our little charges push us to the breaking point and before we know it we are telling them everything we know about them and their parents and their faulty DNA and their inability to rub two brain cells together to produce a coherent thought. What's left is a wound as wide as the Grand Canyon. They hate us and we've proven that we hate them. Game over. Everyone just lost. As professionals we must control our urge to blast students with verbal garbage that can scar them for the rest of their lives.

If you've ever had a mean teacher you distinctly know what that feels like and how it sapped every ounce of motivation you may have had every time you entered their classroom.

I remember how Mr. Steeple, my ninth-grade English teacher scolded me in front of the whole class after I didn't pass a test: "Just because you hate the teacher, Ms. Shields, doesn't mean you have to fail your test." I was embarrassed and humiliated and wanted to run as fast as I could from that classroom. I just stared at the graffiti-filled desk and heard a few snickers emanate from the back of the classroom. That added to the humiliation. After class a few friends tried to console me but it didn't work. I felt hurt and dejected and all alone. I didn't tell my mom because I didn't want anyone to know. I just wanted it all to go away. I thought if I pretended it didn't happen then it really didn't happen. I was a model student who didn't deserve to be treated that way. I still feel the remnants of that embarrassment more than 39 years later.

I now have a word for what he did to me. It's shame, and by not telling my mom I allowed it to grow and fester for all of these years. In her bestselling book *I Thought it Was Just Me But it Isn't*, Brene' Brown writes, "We use shame as a tool to parent, teach and discipline our children. Shame is a silent epidemic. It's a problem of epidemic proportions because it has an impact on all of us. What makes it "silent" is our inability or unwillingness to talk openly about shame and explore the ways in which it affects our individual lives, our families, our communities and society. Our silence has actually forced shame underground, where it now permeates our personal and public lives in destructive and insidious ways."[30]

A teacher often uses shame as a form of discipline, hoping it will stop the behavior but what it does is ruin the student/teacher relationship forever. It's hard to trust someone who has embarrassed you in front of your friends. It's even harder to learn in an atmosphere where you feel afraid and insecure. It's also difficult to be an active learner and eager participant in such an environment.

Shame killed my love for English class. I don't think I ever again talked in that class and it hurt like hell. Not being able to share my thoughts was torturous. I never made eye contact with the teacher and shut down every day I walked into his room. I did the work because I wanted to prove him wrong. That same scrappy spirit helped me years later when a journalism professor at a prestigious university used some of the same techniques to embarrass me by giving me private tutoring lessons in a small closet while all the other students got to go out and cover real stories. He also gave me impossible assignments and then questioned their accuracy. I persevered because I wanted to show him I could do the same work as the other students even though he didn't think I could. I survived, although his shame and doubt left an indelible mark on my writing abilities that took years to overcome.

Shame hurts only if one allows it to live in silence. Words have power and they change lives— sometimes for the better—and have the power to leave lasting scars we teachers may never know we caused.

Classroom management is easily one of the most demanding parts of teaching because it's emotionally exhausting. It requires swift action and the ability to never let them see you sweat. It also demands a good sense of who you are and what you believe in. This also requires you to be impartial yet personal. It's all boils down to building a kind and respectful relationship with every one of your little (or not so little) charges.

It's not easy. It can be hell, yet it's one of the most important parts of the job.

Sheryl A. Shields

We get to model how we want our students to behave. We can't tell them they can't use their cell phones in class when we don't adhere to the rule. It's demonstrating integrity by modeling how we expect them to behave in any given situation. It's also important that we allow them to voice their opinions and frustrations in a calm and orderly manner whenever possible. Everyone wants to be heard and know that their opinion matters. It's in times of conflict when we need to listen and understand that there's more than one side to every story. It also helps if we are consistent with our rules. We can't allow certain students to come to class late or have special privileges that aren't afforded everyone. I heard a story of a teacher who was fired because he allowed certain students to run errands for him during class. When other students began to complain he embarrassed them in front of the whole class. They retaliated by telling their parents who informed the principal of the teacher's inequitable actions and spiteful words.

As instructional leaders we have to be responsible for our words and our actions. Just as we hate to be treated differently from our colleagues we need to insure that we aren't doing that to our students as well.

Rita Pearson's Ted Talk video is a must-see for every teacher. In it she explains, "Kids don't learn from people they don't like." She's absolutely right. I've heard hundreds of students complain about teachers they hate, and I often try to coax them into finding one thing they like about the teacher in order to start a dialogue in which they can build a relationship of trust and mutual respect. Most times I fail. Sometimes I'm able to get them to understand how they will most likely lose the power struggle thus cementing a failing grade. Most don't care. Their minds are made up and no kind of cajoling can get them to understand the importance of building a relationship with the enemy. It is guerilla warfare, and they're intent on winning—no matter what the cost.

Classroom management all boils down to three things:

➡ Students need to feel like they have a voice—if they speak up they will be heard.

➡ There has to be a reasonable expectation that the rules won't change from day to day.

➡ Everyone should be treated the same (although it's almost impossible). It's worth the effort.

Effectively managing your class is worth the time and effort because you'll eventually have a classroom filled with kids who understand you and your story while you understand theirs. It gives you a way in which to communicate and connect with them that transcends teaching and learning. You get to model positive relationships and teach more than your content. You get to be kind and respectful which is something some kids never experience at home. Teaching is a way of sharing your love of learning with students in a way no one else can.

Managing Crisis: Yours and Theirs

Life happens every single day whether we want it to or not. Dealing with it in an appropriate way can help relieve the guilt and stress associated with these major life changes, be they welcomed (getting married, having a new baby), or a total surprise (an unexpected illness or death of a family member).

Since I started teaching more than 15 years ago I've moved twice, got divorced, had two kids graduate from college, lost a parent, started a small business and had at least six students pass away. All of these changes have been stressful in a variety of ways and I'm grateful I had a support system and life-coaching training to help me navigate though most of them.

The most recent tragedy involved two students who were murdered by their father on Super Bowl Sunday.

I found out after an administrator alerted us to check our email a few minutes after school started. I sat in utter shock. Luckily, my co-teacher didn't know the students and was able to continue teaching the lesson while I tried desperately to process the irrational thought that told me to run as fast as I could to my car and drive home. After about 20 minutes I was able to gather my composure and decided to stay at work for the rest of the day. Both students, a brother and sister, were in my eighth-period class and I knew I needed to be there for my students in that class.

I somehow made it through the day and my eighth-period class without breaking down. Seeing the sadness and disbelief in their eyes as the counselors tried to console them was more than I could bear at one point, and it took every ounce of willpower to control my emotions.

All I wanted to do was hug every kid in class but I didn't.

Instead I taught a modified version of the lesson I had taught earlier in the day.

It was mentally exhausting and heartbreaking reading the circumstances of their death. I knew I'd never be able to teach this class the same way ever again.

I knew I had to address our loss and help my students understand what had happened and provide a safe place for them to share their feelings. I knew I had to figure out various ways in which we could begin the healing process.

I've lost students before but never like this so I knew we needed to take it easy for the first few days as we reviewed for a test. Of course the majority of the class failed the test. I knew why and decided to curve the grades. I explained that two really special people wanted me to give them a gift. Some understood it right away and quickly explained it to their clueless classmates. They seemed to appreciate the sentiment and I knew that one little gesture would begin the healing process we all needed to go through.

During those first few days I relied heavily on my coaching skills to stay grounded and remain calm when all I wanted to do was cry my heart out.

The Four Square Change Cycle

I knew we were knee-deep in **Square One**—the four-square change cycle created by Dr. Martha Beck, and detailed in her book, *Finding Your Own North Star: Claiming the Life You Were Meant to Live*.[31] She's one of the best life coaches in the business. Not only does she write an informative column every month for Oprah's magazine but she has authored eight insightful books.

The change cycle consists of Square One: Death and rebirth; Square Two: Dreaming and Scheming; Square Three: The Hero's Saga; and Square Four: The Promised Land.

Square One happens when you experience a major change or shift in your life. It could be a life-changing event like graduating from college, getting married, getting divorced, having a baby or suddenly losing a loved one.

I remember vividly joking with Trisha the Friday before she was murdered just as distinctly as I remember reading the email notifying me of her passing. Both memories will forever be etched in my memory. The exact moment I saw her and her brother's names in the email two things happened almost simultaneously: My heart felt like it had just been ripped out of my chest and I knew I had begun my difficult journey through Square One.

I knew running out of the classroom and screaming at the top of my lungs would help ease my intense pain and suffering but it would most likely not be the most professional thing to do in this situation. I immediately went into life-coaching mode and began to take deep breaths as I fought back the tears and sadness that totally consumed every inch of my being. I knew I couldn't hide my emotions so I just sat there motionless while my co-teacher started teaching. After about 20 minutes I was able to contribute to the lesson. By taking the time to realize what had happened and how it had so profoundly shook me to my core allowed me to process the whole event, one moment at a time, and allowed my students to do the same.

Teaching my students how to grieve, and allowing them to recognize and name their pain was important at this stage. Some weren't in the same class as the students who died but they were affected all the same. Some students who were normally the best of friends started arguing. Another student became visibly upset when another student sat in a seat that belonged to one of the students who died. It was a whirlwind of emotions, and often I would just stop whatever lesson I was teaching and explain that these are some of the things that happen when we're grieving. I explained it was OK to be sad and that the sadness wouldn't just go away. It was a process that might take a few months or longer depending on how they allowed themselves to process their emotions.

That same advice was for me, too. When grading a stack of papers I came across Trisha's worksheet. It caught me by surprise and I knew I had to take the time to feel the pain of losing her and her brother. It hurt like hell but I felt it and allowed all the sadness to well-up inside me. Only then was I able to draw a big red heart around her name and attach her paper to a cart next to my desk. It was a constant reminder to process the wide range of feelings that would surface, and help my students do the same.

Square One sucks whether you initiate a "good" change such as accepting a new job or moving to a new city or getting a promotion; it's scary and fraught with challenges but what it does is allow you to move from one phase of your life to the next. We've all had Square One challenges and will more than likely have many more during the course of our lives.

Once I knew the vocabulary of this stage of change, I was better able to deal with the huge changes as they surfaced. Knowing this is comforting because I know there's a limited time in this stage of the game.

In order to survive square one we need to remember to

➡ Take life one moment at a time.

➡ Realize that things are different and you are different and that it's impossible to live the life you used to live and by accepting your new situation you're able to move forward in life instead of dwelling on the past.

Square Two: Dreaming and Scheming

You know you've moved out of Square One when you begin to see things differently. For me it meant I didn't constantly feel a sudden urge to cry when I walked into my eighth-period class. When every student was finally able to laugh at some silly insignificant incident in class I knew we had entered Square Two. Another signal you've crossed the threshold is that you want to do things you've never done before which often includes getting a new wardrobe or hairstyle. I personally love this stage because I get to make things look new and pretty—including me on occasion. This is a time to let yourself dream big. Just know that there are those who love to dash your dreams so it's a good idea to be selective with whom you share your new-found goals and dreams.

In Square Two you get to look at your life and your current situation in a different way and it doesn't hurt as much and you're a lot less afraid to move forward in life. After you've defrosted your dreams and realized you want to do things differently, it's time to put these lofty dreams and goals into action—that's when you cross over into the next phase of the change cycle.

During Square Two it's important to:

➡ Allow yourself to dream. It's OK to daydream about places you'd like to go or what your ideal mate looks like after ending a relationship.

➡ Realize it's OK to laugh and smile and enjoy your life. Most times after experiencing a traumatic event we think we'll never ever laugh again or enjoy our life without him or her. We may even refuse to enjoy anything fun or engage in activities we love.

➡ Remember, you get to do things differently now. It's OK to cut your hair or dress differently. You get to experiment with a new way of living that feels more authentic. It's an easy way to ease into a new way of being and living in the world.

Square Three: The Hero's Saga entails lots of trial and error. It's the place when you put every ounce of effort into a goal or dream only to fall short time and time again. It's named this for a reason. In every good movie the hero/heroine faces lots of obstacles on his/her way to finding true love or the ideal life, and that's exactly what happens here.

Every time I thought I figured out a way to help my students process the sadness we were all experiencing, it backfired. Luckily I knew this would happen; it made me more determined than ever to help them understand that grief is a process and not a static state of being.

It's like that with most aspects of your life as well. Just when you think you've figured out how to please your spouse or significant other something goes just a little wonky which leaves you even more perplexed. That's Square Three. Or what about the time you thought you had tamed your most difficult student only to have her flip you off because you simply asked her to sit quietly? That's Square Three. One day it's all puppies and rainbows and the next it's World War III.

To be perfectly frank, Square Three is a bitch.

It's hard and difficult and makes you want to raise the white flag and just give the heck up.

But don't, because you'll forever be stuck in the purgatory of defeat just steps away from victory.

I think this is what happens to burned-out teachers. They just give up thinking it will never get any better than this and so it doesn't. It's a self-fulfilling prophecy that makes Monday mornings unbearable. It's like dying a slow death because you can't fathom the thought of trying just one more thing.

Yet try you must—by figuring out what you really want and creating a series to teeny-tiny steps to achieve your goal. Then you get to reward yourself when you achieve one of these tiny steps. It's kind of like bribing your students to read a certain passage or write a few sentences or just being able to follow the dotted lines in kindergarten. It's like you're going to give yourself a gold star—only your gold star is something tangible like your favorite treat or dessert or setting up a playdate with one of your most favorite people in the world. Whenever I've mastered a teeny-tiny step I allow myself to buy a book or sometimes I save up my rewards for a larger purchase like a piece of jewelry or a gift card to one of my favorite stores. It's the little things like this that keeps you moving towards your desired goal no matter how many times you seemingly fall flat on your face.

During Square Three it's important to:

➡ Stay focused on your goal. Most likely it's going to get worse before it gets better but it will most assuredly get better.

➡ Moving toward any goal brings its fair share of challenges and rewards. Your goal is to stay the course knowing that someday you'll accomplish whatever it is your heart desires—— even if it's just making it to Christmas break or the end of the school year.

➡ Make sure you're able to temper these difficult times with lots of playdates. Grownups need to make time to have fun with their favorite people who make them laugh and bring great joy just as much as kids do. Research shows that play actually reduces stress and gives you something to look forward to when it's difficult to get out of the bed some mornings.

Square Four: The Promised Land

On the last day of school I gave my last final to my eighth-period class. After everyone was done and all of the donuts were consumed, we laughed and took selfies and I allowed them to follow me on Instagram. I don't normally do this but I felt this was the right thing to do with this group of kids who had gone through so much. I told them the only pictures they would see me post were those of my dogs and a few other quirky things I came across during the summer. I also explained that once school started I was professionally obligated to unfollow them. They agreed.

At that moment I realized we had passed through the first three squares of the change cycle. We had overcome shock and anger and grief. We figured out how to cope as a class and we faced quite a few obstacles to get to this time and place. Just before the bell rang to signal the official end of the school year I told them that I was honored to be their teacher and I was proud of each and every one of them for going through the difficult challenges we faced the past few months. As I fought back the tears and the huge lump in my throat I explained that I didn't know how we'd make it through the last few months but we did and for that I'll be forever grateful to them for teaching me the true meaning of bravery. As the tears started to roll down my cheeks the bell rang and I wished my little charges a safe and happy summer break. We had each earned the right to play and laugh and create memories. After they left my classroom and filed onto the busses that would officially mark the beginning of their summer break I realized that we, each in our own way, would enjoy our own Square Four life.

Cheri Troy: How Breast Cancer Led to a Happier Life

Cheri Troy, a retired Spanish teacher knows all too well how the change cycle works and I'm grateful for her story.[32]

Back in 1996 I was in Mexico for the summer, with my daughter who had just taken a job at a language school. One day, the news came that my mother-in-law had suddenly passed away. I decided to cut my vacation short and go home. If I hadn't, I might not be here today to tell my story.

I was the kind of woman who pushed my health to the side, taking it for granted. With that said, I'll honestly confess that I was going to skip my mammogram that year to be with my daughter, knowing full well that I wouldn't get it done for another year. The week after my mother-in-law's funeral I had the mammogram.

I knew something was wrong as soon as the mammogram was taken, by the look in the technician's eye. I heard the radiologist and technician talking in the next room; I was told I needed to see a specialist. I knew something was wrong. I had a biopsy and one week later it was confirmed: I had breast cancer.

I walked around in a state of shock, angry at everything and everybody, but mostly with my own body that had always been so healthy and now had betrayed me. I had this horrible disease called cancer. I wanted to run away to anywhere but where I was. I even asked the breast surgeon what happened to the women who never came back to see him after their diagnosis. He said yes, there were always some who never returned. I wanted to be one of them. I wanted to hide and pretend that this wasn't happening to me. But I didn't. I stayed. For six agonizing weeks as I awaited my surgery, I read voraciously to learn everything I could about my condition. I wondered which one of the surgical options suggested was the best for me. But most of all, I wondered if I would die.

October 22, 1996 was the date of my surgery. The day before, I took a leave of absence from my high-school teaching position. It was so hard to say goodbye to my students. How do you tell teenagers that you have breast cancer? I didn't want them to worry about me. Many people, including my boss, were crying. In fact, I think I was the only one who didn't break down that day. I seemed to have a superhuman strength, but now, looking back, I know it was the will to survive. I needed to conserve all my energy for the surgery I would face the next day.

The next day was a blur. Things happened so fast. I was wheeled into the operating room and that's the last thing I remember until I woke up more than 10 hours later and couldn't talk.

At first I thought I was dreaming. My family was there, but the best part was … I slowly realized that this was for real. I was alive. I survived. Now I was sure of it. I had been given a second chance to live. I had so much time to reflect as I rested and recuperated and let my body do its healing work. I came to realize that cancer could be a death sentence or a life sentence, positive or negative, depending upon what a person chooses to do with their life after cancer. I began to send my body messages to live; I realized that I had been allowed to live because my job here on this planet was not yet done. There was more for me to do, but I didn't yet know what it was. I remembered a quote from a commencement speech given by Oprah Winfrey, "Turn your wounds into wisdom."

Slowly my life began to change. It began with taking a yoga class at my local park. It then led me to California to become a certified yoga instructor, then back to school here in Chicago to receive a degree in Stress Management.

I began to teach yoga and stress management. I opened my own business and I now regularly lecture to groups on topics relating to stress and illness in the context of mind-body-spiritual connection because I came to believe through my own experience that being healthy not only means the physical aspect of health but the psychological and spiritual aspects.

My path led me to become involved with the Susan G. Komen Foundation as a member of the Survivor Committee. My decision to come back to the classroom after my recovery was difficult. I truly believe that without my positive attitude (using yoga, meditation, breathing techniques and eating healthy) I could not have continued teaching high school.

The hardest part about all of it (now over 14 years ago) was leaving my students, leaving some of the programs we had built together, especially our volunteer activities. We won the largest school team trophy for six years in a row at the Susan G. Komen Race for the Cure in downtown Chicago. We started out with a group of 18 students. It grew to 60 the following year and by the time I left, we were up to over 200 students walking, running or volunteering at the race. Faculty and staff supported the kids' entry fees and families and graduates attended as well. It was great!

I still teach college-level Spanish at a local community college as well as English language classes to parents. I also love that I get to mentor younger teachers, teach yoga, travel and spend lots of time with my kids and grandkids.

Cheri Troy has mastered the Four Square change cycle and learned that going through a life-changing illness can change your life in ways you'd never expect.

If you want more information on how to navigate the change cycle I highly recommend reading Finding Your Own North Star by Martha Beck. It's chocked full of exercises and more detailed descriptions on how you too can successfully navigate a successful journey through the change cycle.

CHAPTER 6
HEALTHY MIND AND
BODY PRACTICES

Exercise: Do you move enough during the day?

When I first started teaching fulltime I thought I'd be able to eat whatever I wanted because I'd be constantly on my feet. It seemed impossible that I'd actually gain weight. This faulty belief led to an extra 15 pounds that settled ever so annoyingly around my waist during my first three years of teaching. Slowly my pants became a little too tight to fasten. It was my own personal vanity and refusal to buy a larger size that forced me to look at what I was eating during the course of the school day.

Shortly after a weight-loss group was formed at work I joined, thinking, "I only needed to lose a few pounds." I was extremely shocked when I stepped on the scale and saw the numbers were well over the 150 milestone I'd promised myself I'd never reach. Yet, here I was staring it in the face, wondering how I'd allowed myself to get there.

After the first meeting I browsed the literature thinking I didn't need to lose that much weight. After my second weigh-in I gained a pound and a half and was mortified. "Oh no," I remember thinking to myself. "This won't happen. I'm not going to be the one who gains weight in a contest intended for everyone to lose." My competitive spirit kicked in, big time.

That night I read the brochure and instructional manual from cover to cover. I bought a weight-loss cookbook and groceries for my first week of eating healthier. I didn't tell my family that I was changing the way we ate because I didn't want to make two different meals. They quickly realized what I was up to as I cooked a week's worth of meals for me each Sunday and regular meals for them during the week.

By the end of the challenge I had lost 15 pounds and dropped three sizes. During the course of the challenge I bought my favorite pair of pants in all three sizes and marveled at my ability to change the way I ate and made time to exercise at least three times a week in my basement.

The good news is that I was able to change the portions of my food—and the bad news is that it lasted about a year. As the weight came back I slowly began buying larger sized pants and dresses because I had given all my larger clothes away thinking I'd never need them again.

I used every excuse in the book for not eating healthier and incorporating a regular exercise routine into my life. That is until I turned the big 5-0 and needed a way to cope with the hot flashes without hormone replacement therapy.

All the research and conversations with my doctor led me to one conclusion: exercise. I made a public proclamation on Facebook that I was changing my ways. That lasted a few weeks until my daughter took my credit card and signed me up for a gym membership.

I staged a silent boycott my first month, then realized I was only wasting my money. The second month I began a 30-day, one-woman challenge and made it to day 23 about two years ago.

Once summer rolled around I dusted off my running app (Couch to 5k), which promised to have me ready to run my first 5k in 10 weeks. It worked; I've been happily running ever since. I'm able to maintain the same weight. I've even grown to love going to the gym because I relish in the fact that I just did something that was good for both my mind and my body.

What I've learned is that on the days I exercise after work I feel a whole lot better. I eat less after each workout because I don't want to consume more calories than I just burned. My clothes have begun to fit better and the not so little weight around my waist began to subside. I have no aspirations of someday being a super-model thin; I'm happy with the way I'm consistently incorporating exercise into my life. I wish I had done this from the very beginning of my teaching career. Here are a few ways in which exercise helps reduce the stress every teacher feels on a daily basis:

➡ It makes you feel a whole lot better. Moving your body helps reduce stress by ramping up your endorphins which, in turn, helps you feel better. You can achieve this by taking a leisurely or brisk walk, going for a quick run, playing your favorite sport or simply chasing your kids round the living room. Anything that gets your body moving helps reduce stress.

➡ Focus on something other than work. Something as simple as taking a few minutes to sit quietly and meditate or just zone-out while playing with your kids or your favorite video game helps shed those stress-inducing thoughts.

➡ It improves your mood. Every time you make a conscious decision to move your body to improve your health, you win. The hardest part is setting up a regular routine and sticking to it. When you make plans to go to the gym or workout in your basement three times a week, you're making a commitment to living a healthier life which goes a long way in improving your quality of life now and for years to come. The best part is that regular exercise reduces mild depression, anxiety and lowers your chances of getting Type 2 Diabetes.

One of my favorite parts of exercise is how grateful I feel that I pushed myself after a difficult run. It's knowing I ran just a little farther than I mentally or physically thought I could that motivates me to keep going, no matter how tired I may feel. I also love the amazing ideas and other insights I gain after a long walk. What I have figured out is that doing something I enjoy doing, like learning how to swim and play golf, the more likely I am to exercise. It's about simply finding something you like to do with people you like doing it with.

Ways to Get Motivated to Exercise

Ready to start an exercise program but can't find the motivation to get started? Here are a few questions to help you see what's keeping you from exercising. Turn to **Appendix C** and answer the questions in the section entitled: Ways to Get Motivated to Exercise.

Food: Eating Highly Nutritious Snacks and Meals

A few years ago I started drinking green smoothies and juicing. I also stopped eating beef and only ate pork sausage on my favorite deep-dish pizza. I also tried to eliminate most dairy products from my diet because it made breathing extremely difficult. Of course there were a few exceptions: cheese pizza and Coldstone ice cream, which was just a few steps from my front door. But soon the discomfort I felt after digesting these two delicious treats became too much to handle and I decided to get tested for food allergies. I thought that once I knew for sure what foods caused me problems I'd be better able to choose their more nutritious counterparts. Boy was I in for the shock of my life when I was told I was allergic to almost every food—with the exception of nine: carrots, lamb, rice, wheat, strawberries, tuna, pork, banana and chocolate.

That meant my precious chocolate-covered almonds were out—as well as my spaghetti dinner. I could no longer eat my morning oatmeal or any of my favorite seafood. It basically meant I got to starve a slow and difficult death because my body didn't seem to like anything I regularly ate.

Although I was relieved to know this information, I was also saddened that I could no longer indulge in my weekly diet of chicken salad or chicken sandwich from my favorite local restaurant. It meant I was doomed to a chicken-less diet for the foreseeable future. It was sad and quite scary.

How in the hell was I supposed to feed myself and nourish my body with only nine foods? Did I mention that I gave up pork and never ate lamb? What I realized after a few days of binging on my favorite chicken salad was I could now incorporate a diet filled with things my body liked or at least tolerated while I figured out ways to make a variety of nutritious meals for one.

I was also grateful this discovery occurred in the middle of my summer break because I have no idea how I would have had time to incorporate a brand new way of eating into my life during the school year.

Little by little I lost my craving for all things chicken. I learned how to dine out with friends by first checking the restaurant's menu for anything that closely resembled my nine dietary items. Most of the time I'd eat before I left home and order an appetizer. This kept me focused on getting through the first three weeks of bland living to ensure I'd be "clean" enough to introduce my most beloved items, one at a time.

It was like I was the baby who had to eat one thing at a time and wait for a few days to see whether or not it caused any problems in my little tummy or elsewhere in my body.

I learned I could live without my beloved cookies and cake. I even went to Coldstone with my daughter one night with the intent of just ordering a little bit of ice cream and decided at the last minute to do the right thing. Yes! Yet another victory on my road toward eating food that agrees with my digestive system.

In the past year I've learned that eating foods that don't agree with me brings pain and severe discomfort so I no longer have the desire to eat foods my system can't tolerate. I've learned I was an emotional eater, meaning I would eat when I was bored, when I was upset and when something great happened. I no longer have the desire to do that since what I can eat is still limited. I've been able to incorporate a few more foods and only eat organic turkey meat in my chili when the weather's cold. Another benefit of eating the right foods is weight loss. I've lost over 15 pounds and have been told by my doctor and family members that I look totally different. My daughter pointed out recently the extra neck I used to have is now completely gone. I can see that I've lost a lot of weight in my torso area. I now fit into a dress I bought five years ago for my 30th high school reunion. It's been difficult especially when there's nothing to pack for lunch and I have to run to the local grocery story during my lunch break. Yet, I'm grateful that I get to eat food that nourishes my body and makes me feel a whole lot better.

Hopefully, your road toward healthy eating won't be anything like mine.

Why Stress Loves Sugar—And How to Kick the Habit

I've always considered myself a healthy eater. That is until I started writing this book. Most days I would eat a pack of 100-calorie cookies and a Snapple peach tea during seventh period to reward myself for almost getting through another day. I discovered that my "healthy snack" contained more than twice the amount of recommended sugar (19 tablespoons) and almost half the recommended amount of carbs (96) for women. This wouldn't be so bad if it was the only sugary food I ate during the day but it wasn't. When I tried to eat healthier and ditch the cookies and tea I became irritable during the last period of the day and for the life of me couldn't figure out why.

What I discovered is that by the end of the day I'm normally pretty stressed which increased my craving for sugary foods like cookies and sweet drinks. They made me feel better, and I thought I was choosing a healthy snack. Boy was I wrong. A healthier snack might have been a piece of fruit with natural sugars such as an apple or a piece of citrus fruit.

The American Heart Association recommends women should eat no more than 8.25 tablespoons of sugar[33] and men should ingest nine tablespoons, but the average American eats a little more than 25 teaspoons. That equals three cans of soft drinks per day.

What makes sugar so harmful is that it prevents white blood cells from killing germs and fighting bacteria in the body by 40 to 50 percent. It increases insulin levels, causes high blood pressure, high cholesterol, diabetes, heart disease, weight gain and premature aging. Excessive sugar consumption leads to depression and schizophrenia, according to British psychologist Malcolm Peet.[34]

Now that I know the harmful effects of too much sugar, I get to consciously consume less of it. My weaknesses are cookies, cake and any other sugary treat. One thing I do differently is look for the sugar and carbohydrate numbers on the food and drinks I consume. I absolutely adore iced tea and now limit it to a cup a day until I'm able to successfully kick the sugar habit.

Being conscious of what you ingest on a daily basis can have an amazing effect on your waistline and weight.

Being conscious of what you eat and why you eat it can go a long way in reducing the ill effects of certain foods. Instead of reaching for the sugary or high-carb snack, how about you exercise, call a friend or partake in a hobby? Another antidote to eating healthier foods is examining why you feel drawn to eating certain foods and decoding what void they fill in your life.

By processing the stress in a healthy way (exercising, yoga, journaling, and mediation) you will not only lose the excess pounds, but you will also tune into the things that trigger your craving for sugary foods and drinks.

CHAPTER 7
AVOID UNNECESSARY STRESS
Taming the Time Monster

TIME IS THE ONE COMMODITY there never seems to be enough of these days. It seems as though I'm always running out of it, and the lack of it sends me straight into crazy-panic mode. Once there I focus on all the things I have to do and the lack of time to do it. In this frenzied state I complain and moan and fantasize about throwing a temper tantrum like a two year old in the middle of the main office. Believe me, I would most certainly do it if I knew it would buy me more time.

It would most likely win me a one-way ticket to the nearest psychiatric hospital or land me in the unemployment line—neither of which I want.

Fussing and complaining doesn't work either—it—just exacerbates the problem and leaves us even more frustrated.

Luckily for you there are a few things you can do to grab this insidious monster by his horns and send him on a one-way trip out of your life for good.

I came up with these tips while preparing for a teacher fair because time was not my friend and I wanted to figure out a way to get more of it with a lot less stress.

When you learn to think about time differently, it makes a huge difference in your quality of life and in every area of your personal and professional life.

Faulty Clocks

I've learned that teachers have an inaccurate internal clock that's constantly ticking and it never, ever stops.

Have you ever felt that no matter how much you do there always are 20 other things that need to be done *right now*? This constant dread of never being able to get ahead of the game or just stay current is the number one cause of stress. There are several things you can do to silence the ticking time bomb that seems as though it's about to explode at any minute and destroy everything you've done to keep it under control.

What's underneath the fear?

What's the constant feeling that there's something else you should be doing? The operative word in that last sentence is should. Once you're able to get "should" under control, your battle with time is almost over.

I'll explain the "almost" part in a few minutes.

For now I'd like for you to answer a few questions about the prep that goes into planning a week's worth of lessons. You can substitute more or less time for an instructional unit if that's how you plan your lessons.

How far in advance do you start preparing for a week's worth of lessons?

Do you create a schedule for each task?

Do you have a clear set of tasks that need to be done?

How much time (days, hours, or minutes) do you allot to each task?

How do you feel when lesson planning?

Are there any tasks you enjoy doing more than others?

Do you spend more or less time doing the tasks you don't enjoy doing?

Do you normally complete all of these tasks before you start teaching?

If not, what keeps you from completing everything you wanted to complete?

How do you feel when you don't complete these tasks?

How do you treat yourself when you don't do what you thought you needed to do before your due date?

What do you make it mean when you don't complete a certain task by a certain time or date?

Figuring out what you need to do and then setting a timeframe in which to do it helps tame the frenzied and totally out-of-control time monster because you're able to initiate a realistic plan in which to execute it.

Notice I wrote "realistic" because so many times we set goals that are unattainable, which does nothing but feed the frenzied time monster.

It loves when we wait until the last minute to do a task. It sets off all sorts of self-depreciating thoughts that sends our brains further into fight-and-flight syndrome which is the exact opposite of peace and calm.

Make Realistic To-Do Lists

Most of the teachers I've interviewed during the course of writing this book keep a mental list of all of the things they need to do each day. This creates more stress according to Jill Farmer in her book, *There's not enough time and other lies we tell ourselves.*

She writes, "A freestyler is someone who does not write lists down. Instead, you keep three, four or five lists going on simultaneously in your head. While quick to point out the futility of a to-do list, freestylers are often the most frazzled of us all."[35]

Farmer recommends you create two different kinds of to-do lists.

The first is a two-minute task list that includes anything you can do in two minutes or less. She suggests you include no more than five items and set a timer to complete these tasks. "This is really important. No more than 10 minutes. Not Kidding. Seriously, 10 minutes. Then spend those 10 minutes (or less) doing only the items on your two-minute list. No launching into other things. No "I'll just do this little extra task while I'm here." Stick to your two-minute task list."[36]

Some examples of things to do include:

➡ Check and respond to any important emails

➡ Writing lesson plan objectives on the board

➡ Setting up different learning stations

➡ Checking your office mailbox

➡ Filing extra handouts for absent students

➡ Respond to parent emails

➡ Clean the clutter from your desk

Keep Your Daily To-Do Lists to Five Items or Less

Another important idea from Farmer's book is to keep your daily to-do list to five items. When I first read this I thought, "There's no way a teacher can only have five things on a to-do list." There are normally at least 55 things I need to do during the course of a day and to think that I couldn't have all of those things on my list sent a chill down my spine.

It seemed utterly impossible. I was having no part of this foolishness. That is until I realized the angst and confusion and the mental chaos that kept me spinning in place, wondering what to do next, when it seemed as though there was never enough time to do the simple mundane tasks like get new paper clips from the supply closet. This constant feeling of dread was a part of my life during the school year, every single day.

The thought that I could put only five things on my to-do list was at first terrifying—and then freeing.

It meant I really got to organize my teaching life.

There was no room for scurrying around at the last minute trying to copy handouts for a lesson I was going to teach in five minutes.

It meant planning and photocopying the worksheets for every lesson a week in advance.

That felt good and reduced a ton of stress.

My mood went from frazzled and unfocused to calm and collected. I loved how my whole body felt a lot less stressed.

Farmer writes, "The purpose of your to-do list is not to warehouse all of the angst-producing tasks and duties in your life. It is to help you track and remember action items that you'd like to get done today. To-do lists are for today. You can even call it your to-day list, if that floats your boat."[37]

She also has a suggestion for all the items that don't make it your To-Day list. "Anything with a specific future date goes on your calendar. Tasks that repeat (daily or otherwise) belong on your calendar, assigned to a specific time of day."[38]

The time-of-day part can be difficult and a bit unrealistic for teachers because of fluctuating schedules.

The most important goal is to make a list of your top five items that need to be done each day and only do those.

This can be a difficult task and a real paradigm shift because if you're anything like I am, (and most teachers I've worked with), we think we have to do it all right now. It's as though we think doing something tomorrow makes us less dedicated or effective. It's almost as though we set the bar so high that doing anything less is inconceivable.

I've known colleagues who routinely work 12-hour days. During my early years as a yearbook advisor I did the same, trying to stay afloat of the constant deadlines. I didn't realize the tremendous stress I was under until I gave it up.

I would have scoffed at the idea of placing only five things on my to-do list every day. Doing so would have meant I delegated most of the work to my students and had a lot less on me. One of the objectives of Yearbook class was to teach the students to produce a historical reference of the year by learning how to write headlines, stories and photo captions. They also had to choose appropriate pictures, which sometimes was difficult to teach.

I'm pretty sure I learned a lot more than I taught because I was unable to relinquish the writing and other tasks to my students. Knowing how to delegate would have taught me how to set appropriate time boundaries and made me a much happier person—and a more present parent. It also would have taught me how to create more engaging lessons.

Time is one of your most precious commodities as a teacher. Learning how to manage it in more effective ways lessens your stress level and gives you more time to plan engaging lessons without sacrificing your quality of life.

Einstein Time

Another one of my favorite books on time management is *The Big Leap*, by Gay Hendricks. In it he details a concept he calls Einstein Time.

He writes, "If you get a handle on how time actually operates, your work flows gracefully and at high performance. If you don't, it doesn't. Before I figured out how time actually works, I put in twice as many hours and got half as much done. Everything changed when I figured out the secret of Einstein Time. Now I work half as much and get at least twice as much done.[39]

Now isn't that the goal of every teacher in the world—to work half as much and get twice as much done? Here's how it works:

Remember the day you fell in love with your mate or a special pet? Recall all the specifics details of that day.

Where were you?

What was the weather like?

How did you feel?

How long were you together that day?

Did the time pass quickly or slowly?

Now I'd like for you to remember a teachers meeting you were in.

Did you want to be there?

How did you feel?

Was the topic riveting?

Were you actively engaged or bored to tears?

How long was the meeting?

Did the time pass quickly or slowly?

The premise of Einstein Time is based on this principal: "learning to occupy space in a new way, we gain the ability to generate more time."[40]

"An hour with your beloved feels like a minute; a minute on a hot stove feels like an hour. This example has everything you need to understand Einstein Time and its powerful positive ramifications for how we live our lives. If you are forced to sit on a hot stove, you become preoccupied with trying not to occupy the space you're in. You withdraw your consciousness toward your core, contracting away from the pain of contact with the stove. The act of contracting your awareness away from space makes time congeal. It seems to slow down and harden into a solid mass. The more you cringe from the pain, the slower time gets. When you're in love, you relax into the space around you and in you, and as your consciousness expands into space, time disappears. If you even remember to glance at a clock, you notice that time has leaped forward in great spurts. Entire hours can disappear in the wink of an eye. When your heart is beating in time with your beloveds, your every cell is reaching out for total union."[40]

You forget about time. When you're willing to occupy all space, time simply disappears. You're everywhere all at once, there's no place to get to, and everywhere you are it's exactly the right time."[41]

Hendricks suggests we confront our lack of time by making a few simple, yet profound shifts.

The first involves taking full ownership of your time.

We do that by taking a good look at our time personas. Are you the Time Cop who is punctual to every event or the Time Slacker who routinely runs late?[42]

Einstein Time requires you "take charge of the amount of time [you] have. We realize that we're where time comes from. We embrace this liberating insight; since I'm the producer of time, I can make as much of it as I need! By getting the truth of this statement, we make a major adjustment in ourselves. We are no longer in an 'us versus them' relationship with time. We're the source of time, and by realizing that fact we become the truth of it."[43]

In short, this means you get to decide how you spend your time.

If you want to spend it complaining about all the policies the school board just enacted or the email the principal just sent out, you can.

Just know that you're using your time in a way that's not productive and that you get to use your own personal time to do the things you had on your to-do list.

To dig a little deeper Hendricks poses a few questions to help you realized you're the source of time.

Where in my life am I not taking full ownership? Or what am I trying to disown?[44]

Or:

What aspect of my life do I need to take full ownership of?[44]

The author writes, "… stress and conflict are caused by resisting acceptance and ownership. If there is any part of ourselves or our lives that we're not fully willing to accept, we will experience stress and friction in that area. The stress will disappear the moment we accept that part and claim ownership of it."[45]

Getting honest about your thoughts and concepts of time is imperative to make this important shift. I'll go first:

Hi. I'm Sheryl and I'm addicted to complaining about time. I have a sneaky suspension I'm not the only one. One day I spent so much time twisting my head to look at the clock that I ended up with a sore neck from all the constant turning back and forth and I felt like I needed one of those dreadful looking neck braces to support my aching neck. I decided at the last minute to create a special, one-of-a kind worksheet for my next period class and I need to constantly monitor my time.

With every glance I felt more pressured to finish. Then the printer jammed and the nearest photocopier was out of order. That sent my stress level way over the moon and I realized I might have gotten more done if I relaxed and not spent the whole time whipping my head back and forth, frantically looking at the clock.

In order to take control of time, you need to stop complaining about time. "When you stop complaining about time, you cease perpetuating the destructive myth that time is the persecutor and you are its victim."[46]

Every time you utter the excuse of not having enough time, "you're telling a polite lie to avoid saying 'I don't want to do that right now,'" according to Hendricks.[47]

If you get honest about what it is you really want to do and what you really have to do you can reduce your stress level about time immensely. One way to tap into how stressed you are about time is to figure out how your body processes time pressure by answering the following questions:

When you're late for a meeting or event, where do you feel this in your body?

When you're in a hurry, where do you feel this in your body?

What does boredom feel like in your body?

Once you're able to pinpoint these feelings, you can catch these feelings before they wreak havoc on your mood and your ability to get things done easily and effortlessly. When I think of all the time I've spent complaining about the lack of time, I cringe at the thought of all the work I could have done during the school day instead of lugging it home to do during my free time.

I know this may seem slightly odd and a bit simplistic, but I've seen the wonders of it in action and have vowed to never again complain about the lack of time because doing so places awareness on lack and makes your stress levels rise. Who wants to feel like that at work or at home?

I remember the disbelief of the participants in a seminar I gave a couple of years ago. It was a hard concept to grasp because they, like most teachers around the world, believe that time is our biggest enemy when it's simply our frenzied focus on it that makes this so.

"The original insight—that we are the source of time, that time is not a pressure from outside, that we can make as much as we need—takes only a split second to comprehend. However, it takes a lot of practice to integrate that insight into the practicalities of our lives. The main thing it takes is keen attention. Be on the lookout for complaints about time that come out of your mouth or go through your mind. As you spot them and eliminate them one by one, you will grow steadily less busy while getting a great deal more done."[48]

This one concept has made a huge difference in my life and I'm sure it can do the same for yours.

CHAPTER 8
PERMISSION TO FOLLOW
YOUR PASSION

YOU BECAME A TEACHER BECAUSE OF YOUR LOVE of learning and your desire to share it with others. Some, like Florence, have known they wanted to become teachers since they were little kids while others entered the profession after working in another career. The most important factor relates to why you continue to teach and whether or not that passion fuels your desire to do a good job every single day. If it doesn't, that's perfectly fine. Everyone gets to do work that makes them happy and if teaching no longer fills you up like it used to, it's time to do a little soul searching to find another career that inspires your passion. You get to tap into your original medicine and find the work you were born to do.

As a society we're not taught to tap into that special sense of knowing our life's work. We're often told to go to college and choose a career that pays well. If you had enlightened parents or a progressive thinking counselor in high school you may have been given an "interest inventory" to help you discover your passions. Those sorts of tests didn't exist when I was in high school. It wasn't until I was in my mid-30s that I stumbled across a few books that helped me figure out what I loved doing. Even then, it took me quite a few more years to unearth a brand new field called life coaching. What I discovered is that I had been helping people solve their problems and find their original medicine for years. During my first few years of teaching I created a project to help my students research their chosen careers and then shadow someone working in that field. They wrote an in-depth research paper and gave an oral report on their findings. Seeing them realize that their chosen field wasn't a right fit was amazing. One such discovery prompted a parent to mail a letter explaining how my career research project had saved her family thousands of dollars on a college degree their son would never use. After shadowing his family dentist he discovered his aversion to putting his hands in peoples' mouths all day long. He later realized he wanted to teach high-school English so that he could help the next generation learn to love literature. My intention was to help my students find out what they didn't want to do in hopes of getting them one step closer to tapping into their original medicine, although at the time I had no idea this was what I was doing or what it was called.

Explaining this concept to teenagers who have no idea who they are or what they're interested in can be as difficult as explaining what the color red looks like to someone born without sight. Yet it's one of the most fascinating things I've ever done. Doing work that makes every cell in my body jump for joy is something everyone should experience every day. Each time I sat down to write this book, I had the same sensation. Interviewing doctors and other specialists gave me goosebumps because I knew I was doing the work I was born to do.

Tapping into this inner sense of knowing can be one of the easiest things you've ever done or a complete nightmare, depending on your beliefs about work. Most Americans subscribe to the Puritan work ethic that your job has to be hard work and boring; it's something you have to do to earn a paycheck. There may be occasional moments of joy, but it's just something you do until you retire. End of story.

I must admit I thought the same thing until I became a life coach and met amazing people who have been able to carve out incredibly interesting lives doing work that feels like play. You can too, once you're ready to get clear about a few things.

Step One: Answer a few questions.

1. When you were a teeny-tiny version of yourself what did you want to be when you grew up?

2. List any activity where you lose track of time.

3. If you could have any career, what would it be? Don't worry about not being qualified or having the talent to actually do it.

4. If you only had one year left to live, how would you spend your time? What would you do for fun?

5. Did you ever think you should do a different line of work but didn't because society, your parents, your spouse or other family members thought it was a horrible idea?

The key to tuning into your original medicine is to notice what aspects of your job you love to do and which parts you don't like so much. Once you are able to come up with a list of things you love doing, in and out of the classroom, you get to brainstorm possible careers that include those things. I realized I loved creating assignments that helped students tap into specific skills and interests they had, and then coming up with creative ways to legally earn a living doing it. One incredibly lazy student said his original medicine included sleeping. As a class we brainstormed various careers such as mattress tester, hotel room critic, and a host of other jobs that included earning a living sleeping.

Once you come up with your list of dream jobs, you get to fill out the Dream Job worksheet to see whether or not it's truly something you want to do. Later, you'll talk to family and friends to see if they know anyone who does this kind of work. Then you get to interview them or shadow them to see how you feel being in that kind of environment. Remember, your goal is to feel all goosebumpy. Anything less means you're headed in the wrong direction. Just imagine waking up every morning excited to do work that makes every part of you extremely happy instead of cursing that it's only Monday and there are four more days until the weekend.

I believe that we do a great disservice to our students when we aren't able to share our passion for teaching and learning with them. When we just phone it in, they do the same. When we love what we do, that energy transfers as well. It's in this light that I hope everyone who is called to teach does so in a way that helps instead of hinders the learning process. Students deserve a teacher who wants to teach instead of someone just biding their time until retirement. A few days ago I went to a new doctor who was kind and compassionate and extremely attentive. She asked questions and listened patiently to my answers. She was efficient and professional. I'll most likely be a patient until I move or she retires. I knew within the first few minutes that she loved what she did and had my best interests at heart. It was one of the shortest appointments I have ever had; I left grateful for the experience.

Wouldn't it be wonderful if all of your students left your class this way? It may not be realistic every single day, but what if it were? I'm sure I had that amazing experience with my doctor because she was tapped into a source of joy, and providing a service made her extremely happy. You've felt it when you've received exceptional service from someone, and that's a good standard to aim for with students. Doing so makes me Emotionally happy or, as I like to write it, happE.

When you do work you were born to do, and use all of your unique gifts and talents, you help others in a way that no one else can. I work with burned-out teachers because I know what it feels like to secretly hate going to a job that makes you feel incompetent. Doing so helps me combine lessons I learned from that painful experience with my life-coaching expertise to help teachers transition from a job they hate to one they are able to fall in love with again or find another profession where they can use their original medicine every single day.

One person who has done that brilliantly is Michael Trotta. We first met at a life-coaching conference several years ago. I'm grateful he agreed to share his story about how he transitioned from education to becoming a fulltime life coach and wood carver.

Michael Trotta's Story: Coaching Others to Tap Into Their Original Medicine

For eight years Michael Trotta taught Special Education to fifth graders in Westchester County New York.[49] By 2005 he had had enough and took a leave of absence, then extended it an additional year. Now Michael lives his life nurturing his original medicine that consists of carving beautiful wooden animals, teaching people to nurture their true nature by finding theirs much like he did nine years ago. Here's how he made the transition by following his original medicine to help others find theirs:

I felt I could impact more people in a bigger way by teaching without the restrictions of a public school, which left me wanting more time for my family, and myself.

Leaving a steady income wasn't an easy thing to do. I had just bought a house and I had no idea if the nature-based mentoring programs I had created were going to be enough to support us. The fears didn't go away. I went ahead anyway.

Taking the time off gave me a little breathing room and ultimately, I was able to make the same amount of money from my business ventures, in a lot less time, doing something I completely loved.

Now I'm a Master Coach, a consultant and a mentor who owns and operates Sagefire Institute. It was created because I saw a very real need in our culture. As an educator, it was clear to me that curriculum driven learning was failing to acknowledge and connect individuals to their gifts and talents. As a result, many children learn to ignore their truth as well as their genius and thus, spend their lives feeling that something is missing.

As I studied how native, earth-based cultures educated their children, I quickly understood that the focus was not on curriculum but rather, on connecting individuals to those things that made them special, to their Original Medicine, and to help them discover how they might use their medicine to serve The People. This was not just some nice cultural experiment. This was a very real survival requirement: each person living from their Medicine and using it to serve the greater community. It has been said that, a person not living their vision is not truly living and a tribe of people not truly living does not last long, let alone thrive. Today, our children are more disconnected than ever. Adults too, find themselves "stuck" in jobs and relationships that do not feed them.

I also work as a literacy coach, helping teachers to build healthy classrooms while guiding them in balanced literacy instruction which I believe is a method of instruction that is congruent with healthy classrooms. I work as an artist— making and selling wood sculptures that mark important moments in a person's life (*www.RMTrotta.com*).

What I love about my current job is that, I largely get to make it up as I go along, constantly sharing my creativity and love of nature with others while helping them do the same for themselves. In this, I am never bored, I always feel in integrity with my beliefs (something that I often did not feel teaching), and while I am very busy, its largely doing things I would do if it were my own time, which I guess it is, so I win!

Some days it's my dream job and some days it isn't. But unlike when I was in the classroom, it continually evolves and I can take full responsibility for when it is and is not a dream. When it's not I simply try something else. The diversity of my work helps with this.

Honestly, it would be easy to say teaching is the main skill I use from my former career. But my skills as a teacher do not come from my work in schools nor do they come from graduate school where I was taught to teach. So to be honest, I use very little of what I used in my teaching career with the exception of the knowledge of balanced literacy that I did learn while working in a school. Thinking on it, another reason I left, was because the good teaching practices that I had acquired largely from learning from native elders and nature based cultures, was limited by the structure of the modern school system. I tried for years but ultimately felt stifled, like I was forced to be less than I was so to speak.

Changing careers proved difficult in a few areas because I was always working on something that I was interested in which was great! A big shift I had to make was around being a business owner. This required some work, as I was accustomed to having my students assigned to me. Now I had to go find them and get parents and later adults to understand how what I was offering them was worth paying for.

My biggest challenge after leaving was the loss of my identity as a teacher. I loved being a teacher I just didn't like the system. So when I left, I struggled with an answer to "So, what do you do for a living?" I had left something that most people understood and could conceptualize for a completely made up profession - nobody was doing what I did the way I did it. And no title seemed to fit - executive director, business owner, CEO, even teacher felt wrong because people couldn't understand that I was a teacher without a school. I still struggle with this but it's not painful for me the way it once was. Now, I typically tell people I am a coach/consultant (whatever that means). It doesn't feel like it says anything that I identify with but for people who ask the follow up, 'What do you coach?' I normally come up with something that feels right for the situation.

If you're looking to leave the profession like I did, I advise you to use the system to support you while you prepare yourself. Do your job, of course, and make the mental switch to see that this job can provide you with the resources that will allow you to prepare for what's next. The leap will always feel like a leap, but it doesn't hurt to leap smart.

My wife and I now run a thriving business leading others towards living their right life. A few years ago, I got a call from Martha Beck, bestselling author and monthly contributor to Oprah's magazine. She invited me to participate in something called the Purpose Project. It never went beyond the beta test but in many ways birthed the STAR retreats (Self-Transformation Adventure Retreats) and Nature-based Coach Training program that was written by me and originally offered through Martha Beck International to host a weekend workshop. A recent offshoot of that was the Escape from the man cave, a weekend workshop for men. This program garnered national press in the New York Times last December.

When we are able to tap into our unique gifts and talents we are able to help people in a way that brings great joy and love to you and them.

CHAPTER 9
PLAN FOR ANOTHER CAREER

I met Pam Slim more than eight years ago at a coaching conference in Chicago. Her quick wit, generous soul and kind demeanor were immediately apparent in her break out session geared towards helping newbie coaches like me succeed. Since that time I've read her blogs, bought a few of her programs and read her books. Her first bestselling book, Escape from Cubical Nation, was published in 2009, and I didn't read it until two years ago after searching for business books to help me transition from teaching to being a fulltime entrepreneur. I mistakenly thought it was written for people who worked in big corporations, not teachers. Boy was I wrong. In it I learned how to set up my business, shop around for health insurance and grow my business while still teaching fulltime. It's an invaluable asset in helping anyone who wants to transition from one career to another create a timeline to do just that. When her second book, Body of Work, was published almost two years ago I immediately downloaded it because I couldn't wait three days for it to be delivered by mail. I read it cover-to-cover in just three days. It contains a wealth of information on doing work you love:

"Your body of work is everything you create, contribute, affect, and impact. For individuals, it is the personal legacy you leave at the end of your life, including all the tangible and intangible things you have created. Individuals who structure their careers around autonomy, mastery, and purpose will have a powerful body of work."[50]

Teachers often think their body of work is simply teaching when it's so much more than that. In its simplest form it's the ability to transfer information from one source to another; it can be used in writing, public speaking, publishing, creating innovative ways in which to solve problems and countless other careers. I learned that my knowledge of photography, print and broadcast journalism, substitute teaching and being a stay-at-home mom contributed greatly to my teaching career. Because of my journalism degrees I was able to teach Yearbook and later started the Television Production program at my school. My love of writing makes it easy to help struggling writers learn new ways in which to express themselves. My life coaching experience helps me create lessons that incorporated resilience while motivating students to use their unique gifts and talents. My passion for helping people do work that feels like play helps my coaching clients transition to work that inspires instead of depletes. All of these experiences not only made me a better teacher but also contributed to my body of work to help people live happier lives, which is one of the main intentions of this book.

When you look at your life experiences as a whole, you can see how teaching can be just one part of a career dedicated toward helping others learn. Knowing this can help ease the pain of saying goodbye to a career you may have dedicated yourself to for years. Leaving the classroom can be one of the hardest decisions any teacher can ever make, and it also can be one of the best. Thousands of teachers resign every year for a wide variety of reasons. When the thought of teaching another year feels like you've been sentenced to a 10-year prison term, you know it's time to take a long hard look at what you do and why you believe you still have to do a job you hate. As you've learned in the previous chapters, doing so can be detrimental to your mental and physical health. However, it doesn't have to be that way. Here are a few more stories of brave souls who chose to leave the classroom, and one who returned to the classroom after years as an administrator.

Kaitlyn Leach's Story: Teaching All Around the World

Kaitlyn Leach taught English and Yearbook in a suburban Chicago high school for three years before teaching abroad in Brazil, South Africa, and Turkey.[51]

Here are the top five factors that contributed to her leaving her former teaching position, and her story:

1. I always knew that I wanted to teach overseas, so even though I loved my first teaching job, I wanted the experience to live overseas.

2. I was working two other jobs besides teaching high school, and I was still paycheck to paycheck. I wanted to be able to focus on only one job.

3. Class size at public schools in the states made our job more difficult and made improving student writing close to impossible.

4. I felt that as teachers we were often pulled away from just teaching to worry about Individual Education Plans, state tests, everything other than the main focus of student learning.

5. Not to mention the behavior problems that I often encountered in my classroom, some of which included fighting.

I wanted to teach in another country because I wanted an international experience like my parents and grandparents had. I also felt that I would be a more open-minded teacher if I left my comfort zone and continued to learn about the world by setting up a life over and over again in different places, which tapped into my love of traveling. Financially it seemed to make sense.

The application process is not very difficult, but you have to start early. Interviews for the following school year start in October. The best way to set yourself up for success is to register with one of the following recruitment agencies. Each school is an independent private school and the two agencies below connect the schools and the teachers together. They collect numerous documents, check your references and help you create a profile, which is available to all the schools. They also list all the openings and details on each schools background, package, and population.

Recruitment Agencies:

➡ www.searchassociates.com

➡ www.iss.edu

Independent School Fairs

➡ www.aassa.com

➡ www.uni.edu/placement/overseas/

My husband and I currently work for a private Turkish high school. It is considered one of the top five high schools in Turkey and students need to do exceptionally well on the national Turkish exam to be admitted.

The best part about teaching abroad is being able to travel extensively in different areas of the world, affordably. I could have never taken the trips I took on an American teacher's salary traveling from the States. I wouldn't have had the time off. I wouldn't have known where to go. We learn so much about a culture. Most of the spots we visit are off the tourist's grid, which makes our travels and experiences unique.

The worst part about teaching in another country is we have to give up of friends, family, and our stuff and set up our life over and over again in new places—completely out of our comfort zone. Very few people speak English, and we need help with everything. There is always a bit of a honeymoon period at a new location, but soon it wears off and the struggles ensue. All of our ideologies come into question when very few people at our new location see the world and education the way we do. We are forced to change and to adapt, which is good in some ways, but it changes us, and soon there is more than just physical distance between us and those back in the states.

Another downside is that the people at home also don't want to know about our life overseas. If we start telling a story most often people just try to change the subject or their eyes glaze over. Now when we come home we realize it is to listen to the tales of our friends and families and keep a lid on our stories.

There are lots of rewards to teaching overseas, but in no way is it easier than teaching in the states. Many people try and move back home after their first contract or even sometimes break contract and leave early.

Lastly, we never have a home of our own. Sometimes when we go back home, Kurt and I dream of the house we might buy if we had continued to work in Chicago.

I love that that my apartment is a five-minute walk to my classroom door. This is a first for us and it has been a wonderful perk. The school also allows us to come and go when we don't have class, which is really nice. I love teaching the International Baccalaureate (IB), and now we only choose schools that offer us IB assignments.

Schools are unofficially ranked into three tiers. Tier three schools are a major mess. Ending up at one of these schools means little organization, sometimes it is even difficult to get your paycheck. To avoid these schools, it helps to look at online reviews: www.internationalschoolsreview.com

➡ Tier Two schools are good schools, where you can learn a lot and grow as an educator. The packages are average, but good, and the schools are located in relatively interesting locations.

➡ Tier One schools—our current "dream" school—are considered the best schools in the world. The packages are amazing, but the workload is intense. There are about 15 schools that fit into this category and they are incredible competitive.

➡ Other than that there are a few schools with good packages in prime locations, that would also be a dream, but it seems like you need an in to even be considered, which includes places like Buenos Aires.

The scariest part about teaching in a foreign country is not being around when your family needs you the most. We miss out on a lot, and it would be devastating if someone we love faces tragedy and we are not there to support them.

I guess the same thing applies for us as well. It is scary to go through life without any support system. While I can talk to my family online, I have had a baby and surgery in a hospital where I didn't understand anything that was happening.

We are always thought of as tourists no matter how long we live in a place; we are the outsiders, which can make some situations very difficult. We are often considered in the wrong before the situation is even unveiled, so we are usually skeptical of everything and everyone.

To overcome these fears we've built a support system of expats in each place we move and have local friends on speed dial to help us if we get into a situation, in which we don't feel comfortable.

Our lives are different now because we're minimalists. Since international moving is not cheap, we have learned to live without so many things. When we come back home for the summer it seems like people are often obsessed with things, and we have moved past that. During Christmas we rarely ever exchange gifts. Some find this very odd, but I don't need anything and can't even come up with a list of things I want. Stuff starts to feel like more of a burden, than an asset.

We see the world and particularly America very differently. An international perspective has taught us that a national health care system is so important. We have had better free health care in every other country we have lived in than the health care we paid for in the States.

We have loved teaching in all of our assigned countries and South Africa was our favorite. I loved driving through the wild rolling hills of numerous national parks, as well as eating incredible food and enjoying the local wine. It was also very affordable to live there.

It is a wonderful life we live, and I can't see us turning back anytime soon, but there are sacrifices that we make to have this life.

Because most of the contracts are only for two years I would advise teachers to go for it! In two years you can always move back home.

Don't limit yourself to one specific region of the world. Look at all the options and places. We have never left a job fair with a job we imagined getting when we arrived, but each place has been a perfect fit for us. It is important to go into this career with an open mind.

Lastly there is no teacher pension for international educators. Many schools will give you an additional 10 percent for retirement. This will be either invested into a school set up mutual fund or just given as additional pay in your check, which means planning for retirement is something you have to do on your own. We are able to save much more as international teachers than we were ever able to in the states, but this is also because we choose countries where it is inexpensive to live.

Christina Schulz's Story: Teaching in a Bigger Sense[52]

Fifteen years ago Christina Schulz left the teaching profession after two years for a variety of reasons. We met during a teacher induction meeting and became fast friends. I was saddened by her decision to leave but understood her desire to live a different life in another part of the state. Here's her story:

I taught five sections of English One in an interdisciplinary, team-teaching block-schedule program at a south suburban high school in Chicagoland.

The five factors that contributed to me leaving the teaching profession were:

1. **Quality of life:** The location of my apartment did not lend well to spending time outside, so I spent lots of my non-teaching time indoors, either in my apartment or in stores since there weren't many other destinations to go to near where I lived. The physical geography of my first 'home' after college was just way too different from my life up to that point. I learned in this part of my life how much I had taken for granted access to the outdoors growing up, and it was through my time living in Cook County that I realized how much I needed outdoor activities to countermand

124

the effects of a (literally) mindful profession, such as teaching English.

2. **Emotional and physical isolation:** South suburban Chicago was a new location for me, with no friends or family in proximity. I struggled to get time with family and friends who lived in other suburbs. Similar to my aha moment about my need for outdoor-access, I learned in this post-college period that I did not have the necessary emotional support system to help me manage the emotional volatility that comes with being a new teacher, particularly a new teacher who finds herself facing greater academic challenges on her students' behalf than she had prepared for.

3. **Quality of life:** Hours spent teaching, preparing for lessons, and grading ate up most of my time seven days a week. I literally had no work/life balance. And, as mentioned above relative to isolation, I had difficulty managing visits to friends and family farther away than Cook County, even though many of them were dispersed elsewhere across the Chicagoland area.

4. **Job market:** Upon deciding to relocate to a community that I determined to be both more livable and emotionally supportive, I began a job search in another part of Illinois. What a challenge that proved to be! I found out the hard way that it is much harder to leave a metropolitan community

for a much smaller one than vice versa. In 2001, the opportunities for interviews were slim, and I did not get a teaching position. No one in that part of Illinois was doing interdisciplinary team teaching, and we were only one school in the area at the time was doing block system. I really freaked out one of my interviewers when I described what we did, especially the Reality-Based Learning (RBL). It's funny to me now, and, I must admit, I was pretty relieved not to have been hired at a school that was just way too traditional compared to what we were doing with our kids and colleagues.

5. **Network and naiveté combined:** I believed merits were assets and under-appreciated the value of a professional network. (And, in my early 20s, what amount of professional network could I have really had?) I did not know how to get "inside'" a school system in order to have some advantages to work in my favor, to help my resume rise to the top, or to help create name recognition through people with whom I had an acquaintanceship or friendship. I would recommend anyone studying to be a teacher to learn about networking early and hone those skills. In college, I attributed "networking" to a business skill set, not one for teaching or the professions focused on altruistic values.

I currently work at the Hile Group as a Senior Performance Consultant, where I have been since 2001. It is what I call teaching with a "t" instead of a "T." My work is that of servant leadership. I help individuals, teams, and organizations build collaborative and consensus-focused skills that support positive change relative to safety and organizational culture. I absolutely use my teaching skills 100 percent of the time, and I am an example of the meaningful work that can be done with an English degree. Thanks to my two years of experience with colleagues working on RBL projects, I got a real thirst for matching learners up with relevant, challenging, open-ended activities. Teaching the semi-colon started to pale in comparison to pointing out that a student had used one correctly in his or her report that was going to a real stakeholder for review and not just me in a made-up scenario.

I also love that I work in a small company owned by a working mother. I have benefited a lot from having people around me who were carving their own path, choosing to balance work in the world with raising a family. Right now, in fact, our company is comprised predominantly of women, so I have as much support coming from my coworkers as I do my boss.

Variety with purpose is also something I value about my job, although that can be a double-edged sword at times. For me, variety means travel, and there can definitely be too much of that in a month at times. And purposeful work can also be hard to stop, affecting time management. There's no getting around challenges of work-life balance, it turns out, at any age.

The scariest part about leaving my teaching position was leaving my childhood dream behind and the comfort of having imagined what I wanted to be for 20 years... giving that up for the unknown was easily the scariest thing I have ever confronted as a teacher-defector. Combined with that, the unknown about whether the skills that educators develop are truly universal, if what I had studied with an idea to help young people could be as effectively applied to adults.

For every moment of doubt and uncertainty, I tried to notice a moment of success and sure-footedness. Almost 13 years later, I continue to face my fears head on.

My life was a lot different after I left in that I got more sleep. "Sunday" became an actual weekend day, not an unpaid teaching day. A long period of "where do I belong?" set in, though, since I lost all my professional contacts and long-held sense of myself in the decision to enter a consulting position instead of accept another teaching position as I had originally intended to do when I decided to leave my high school teaching position in the fall of 2000. I gained proximity to loved ones and quality of life but had to start all over, in a sense, regarding the sense I had of myself in the wider world and the contributions I wanted to make through paid work. Today, the biggest difference between school teaching and consulting is that I travel. I sometimes still think, "Look at me, at the airport during second period." That movement through a year is still what I find most exhilarating, and sometimes daunting, in contrast with my teaching life.

There's something inherent with how people define a "dream job" as though "it" already exists, and it is just a matter of applying for it and getting it. I have not found that to be the case—what I want to do, feel most qualified to do, doesn't seem to be easily articulated in a specific job description and, so, feels elusive to me. And it is up to someone else to create for you. That, too, I have not found to be the case. If I want to have a job that is a unique blend of teaching, writing, communication, and service, while also making a living wage while doing it, then it's likely a job I will need to create for myself.

Based on my sense that "dream job" is my responsibility to develop and live out, working at the Hile Group is very close to a dream job. We make our workload, word of mouth is typically how new work comes to us. We are responsible for keeping our company going, and that is a distinctly different and more significant responsibility than anything I ever felt as a teacher.

So, yes, it is pretty close to my dream job: Meaningful work that uses many of my talents and hard-earned skills; the opportunity to travel and see places I would not otherwise know about; life experience that is teaching me how to be independent and strong on my own two feet; access to a community that promotes healthy living and service. And, yet, it isn't exactly my dream job: Business is not like education, and I find that it is not easy to let go of that lifelong dream of being a teacher that I carried from age five to 24. What I miss about education is not easily described in words; images of fun stuff sometimes flash through my mind, such as Shakespearean swearing and recreating scenes from the *Odyssey* using sound effects and moving furniture around. And since we have all bought into the idea dream job should be an all-joy kind of professional experience, it can sometimes be hard to reconcile that lightness with the incredibly heavy stress that comes from being a full-time working mother who travels in service to a small company and its support to organizational culture change—often in the context of safety.

My career and sense of self continue to be a work in progress. Determining whether I have arrived at "dream job" status is dependent on whether I can get the balance between relevant-service and personal satisfaction while being realistic about the amount of stress that will come along with any work that is human in nature.

I would say I draw upon a parallel skill set that I used in teaching, including:

➡ Systems thinking

➡ Needs assessment; lesson/intervention modification and adaptation

➡ Instructional design

➡ Teaching and facilitation = both in person, virtually, and through writing (emails and documentation)

➡ Technology integration

➡ Emotional intelligence

➡ Leadership

➡ Communication

➡ Team- and group-building

➡ Assessment and evaluation

➡ Continuous improvement and lifelong learning: both individually and collegially

If you're looking to leave teaching and pursue another career know that any workplace, any profession will be all the better for having former teachers in their midst. Teaching is absolutely something that stays a part of you even after you leave, and there are numerous ways to tap into that part of yourself. You may give up a certain amount of the 'known' in a career change, but you will gain an awareness of yourself that you may not have known to appreciate by staying within the classroom for an entire career. I learned over time that it wasn't the certification, access to kids, or position within a school building that made me a teacher—it was me. And I'm still that me, that teacher, today.

Josh Waldron's Story: The Tough Decision to Leave the Classroom[53]

As the title suggests, I have made the tough decision to leave the classroom for good at the end of this school year.

The decision is a painful one—both personally and professionally. It is also a public one, as I've been honored as recently as last month by the Waynesboro Rotary Club as its 2014 High School Teacher of the Year, my fourth such honor in six years.

In that respect, I feel an explanation is in order, as well as a prescription for what we—as a community—can do to right the ship.

Every workplace has its imperfections and challenges. I accept that. But public education is painted as a career where you make a difference in the lives of students. When a system becomes so deeply flawed that students suffer and good teachers leave (or become jaded), we must examine how and why we do things.

Waynesboro is small enough that we can tackle some of the larger problems that other school systems can't. I want this piece, in part, to force a needed, collective conversation.

In doing so, I don't want to come across as prideful or arrogant. I simply want my neighbors and friends to understand the frustrations at issue and what's at stake for the next round of teachers and students.

When I came to this area in 2008, I believed I would be a teacher for life. My wife and I signed a lease on an apartment we had never seen and arrived only a few days before school started. Words can't really express how excited I was to land a teaching job, work with high school students, and invest in teenagers the way one teacher invested in me.

That first year coincided with the first round of school budget cuts. Salaries were frozen and spending was slashed. This basic storyline has repeated itself for the five years that followed.

Over this time, I've lost my optimism and question a mission I once felt wholly committed to.

I still care deeply about students. I've worked hard to brighten their day while giving them an enjoyable and rigorous environment in which to learn. If this job was just about working with students, I couldn't ask for a better or more meaningful career.

The job, though, is about much more. And I have very real concerns about the sustainability of public education in Waynesboro (and as a whole).

To make a real difference in the lives of students, raise the quality of life in greater Waynesboro, and attract and keep life-changing teachers, we must address five key areas:

1. Tear down the hoops

Our teachers spend far too much time jumping through hoops.

Every year, our district invents new goals (such as "21st Century Skills"), measuring sticks (most recently a "Growth Calculator"), time-consuming documentation (see "SMART goals"), modified schedules (think block scheduling and an extended school day), and evaluations (look in our 72-page "Teacher Performance Plan").

As a district, we pretend these are strategic adjustments. They are not. The growth calculator was essentially brought forward out of thin air, SMART goals are a weak attempt to prove we're actually doing something in the classroom, etc. Bad teachers can game any system; good teachers can lose their focus trying to take new requirements seriously.

These hoops have distracted me from our priority (students). I've concluded it's no longer possible to do all things well. We need to tear down these hoops and succeed clearly on simple metrics that matter.

Over the past six years, I can't remember a time where something was taken off my plate. Expectations continue to increase and we play along until we invent new hoops.

On a personal level, with 100-plus students a year, a growing family, and two side jobs, I can no longer be a good teacher and do all the system expects of me.

2. Have a plan for the future

I stepped into the classroom around the time of a major worldwide recession. As the individuals and institutions responsible for this recession escaped accountability for their actions, school districts like ours went into survival mode.

Six years later, we're still there. We have no plan for the future.

Earlier this year, the school board held its annual budget meeting. I left my second job early to attend and asked board members one simple question: "Is there any cause for optimism?" Each school board member, searching for a silver lining, effectively answered "no" by the time their reasoning caught up with them.

These basic mantras seem to govern what we do:

Just do the best you can.

We need to do more with less.

There's no money in the budget for that.

We're hoping things look better next year.

I don't fault our district for a worldwide economic downturn. I do fault it for how it's handled it. For six years in a row, we've cut, cut, cut. And for six years in a row, students and teachers have paid the biggest price.

When times are tough, human beings and institutions have the rare opportunity to reflect and refocus, to think differently and creatively. But instead of seizing the opportunity and gathering stakeholders for collective conversations and solution building, we've wandered around aimlessly hoping to make ends meet.

We should have a clear plan for sustainability. Instead, we're really just worried about balancing the budget.

When we have a desperate need like football bleachers that have to be replaced, or turf grass that isn't up to par, we somehow find the money. We—through public or private avenues—meet those needs. Why can't we find funds to address the areas that seem more pertinent to our primary mission?

3. Scrap obsession with flawed assessments

I've seen teachers cry over Standards of Learning scores. I've seen students cry over SOL scores. I've seen newspaper and TV reports sensationalize SOL scores. These are all indications of an unhealthy obsession with flawed standardized tests.

SOL tests are inherently unfair, but we continue to invest countless hours and resources in our quest for our school to score well. This leads me to the following questions:

➡ Do we care more about student progress or our appearance?

➡ Why can't we start a movement to walk away from these tests?

➡ Why can't we shift our focus to critical thinking and relevant educational experiences?

It's tough to acknowledge that people in Washington, D.C., and Richmond (and sometimes decision makers in Waynesboro) develop systems and policies that affect my students and me negatively. But as they retire and sail off into the sunset, we're the ones left with the consequences of ineffective measurements and strategies.

Our new teacher evaluations focus heavily on test scores. But while teachers are continually under pressure to be held accountable, there seems to be very little accountability for parents, the community, or district offices.

It's only going to get worse, and it seems that we have no intention of taking a stand or advocating against flawed assessments. Instead, we have submitted ourselves to these tools that misrepresent student growth. It is a game, and it is a game I no longer wish to play.

4. Build a community that supports education

Stop by the high school for a sporting event (and I love sports) and you'll be impressed with the attendance and enthusiasm. Stop by the high school on a parent-teacher night and you'll see tumbleweed blowing through the halls.

If parents and local decision-makers really value education (and there is a small portion of the community that does), student and teacher morale would be much different.

Our school and political leaders must help build a community that truly supports education. A real investment from residents across all neighborhoods and groups would change the climate immensely and allow us to truly tackle the challenges that lie ahead.

Unfortunately, the community seems disengaged with such struggles and more concerned with whether or not we'll ever land an Olive Garden.

Until the community boosts its value of education …

➡ How can we provide high quality to all students?

➡ How can we build strong academic programs that meet student needs?

➡ How can we prepare students to be productive citizens?

➡ How can we successfully partner with parents and others?

If we can't reflect the values of our mission statement, then we need to change our mission statement.

We simply can't move forward when there is such little community connection to our educational goals. And if we can't move forward together, I don't want to tread water alone.

5. Fairly compensate educators

Compensation alone has not pushed me away from education. At the same time, the years of salary and step freezes have taken a toll.

If educators are as valuable as we claim they are (our district website says we "strive to hire and retain quality employees"), then we would make sure we take care of employees and their families. We must fairly compensate educators.

Keeping a sixth year teacher on a first year salary is not looking out for someone who looks out for students. For those like me, there's only a $100 difference in our December 2009 and January 2014 monthly paychecks.

My wife and I live on a very strict budget. We are thankful for the quality of life we enjoy compared to other people in the world and try to keep things in their proper perspective. But the only financial reason I can afford to keep teaching is because of two side businesses and the generosity of family and friends. I'm not the only educator who manages extra work to make ends meet. Here are some efforts we've made to make this job sustainable:

➡ We lived with one car (a car that was given to us) for 4.5 years. During that time, I walked or rode my bike to school to save on gas. We recently bought a second car with money I saved from my web design business.

➡ We rarely eat out and maintain our own garden to cut down on food costs.

➡ We bought a $114,000 house that needed lots of work. This kept our mortgage payments in the $700 range, which is about what it would cost to rent a decent apartment.

➡ We haven't taken a vacation since I started teaching six years ago.

I love Waynesboro. I'm rooting for Waynesboro's success. But there needs to be real, quantifiable change if we're going to create a bright future for everyone.

A love for students and teaching drove me for the past six years. Now I'm watching my own kids grow up and am starting to think more and more about my own family.

What will I have to show for myself 10 years from now when I've missed crucial time with my own kids to barely break even and exist in a place where educators aren't really valued? What happens when I dedicate my life to a place only to discover I'm part of their 10th round of budget cuts?

We need answers. I hope this can move us one step closer to asking the questions that will get us there.

Natasha Alford's Story: A New Way of Teaching[54]

Natasha Alford taught Middle School English in an inner city school for two years before leaving to attend Northwestern University's Medill school of journalism to pursue a career as a broadcast journalist. We met at an alumni networking event and I was grateful for her willingness to share her story in that it might help others who are thinking of switching careers as she has.

The five factors that contributed to me leaving the teaching profession were:

1. Desire for greater impact (as in reaching greater numbers of students/people with my work)

2. Instability within my school district (high leadership/teacher turnover; school politics)

3. Low pay trajectory

4. Disinterest in paperwork aspects of the job

5. Desire to lead (more than within my classroom)

I decided to pursue a career in broadcast journalism because I essentially wanted to be an educator again—but this time with a larger audience. I love the variety in the job; no two days are alike. I love to write, speak and meet new people and I think broadcast journalism is my talent. It's the job I was put on earth to do.

I'm happy with my decision to leave teaching and go back to school, although I miss my students often. I miss being relied upon and being the leader of a community. I miss seeing them grow, and having a front-row seat to their victories and challenge. In journalism, you're a little more independent and as a broadcast journalist you have to focus on yourself more, sometimes in superficial ways. ("How did my hair look in that shot? Am I wearing enough make-up? How do I sound? How's the editing?") School was the best way to transition to the field for me and the Medill network is incredible, so I know I made the right decision.

My dream job is to be an owner of a television/media network and a media personality/show host. I want to pick up where Oprah leaves off.

The scariest part about leaving my teaching position was perhaps that I was making a mistake or letting my students down. I feared that the special thing I built with my students would be lost forever. But the reality is that nothing stays the same. Students change from year to year no matter what and if you want to stay in touch with your students, you can and will—and vice versa.

To overcome those fears I moved forward. You can blame it on my young impulsive nature, but when it comes to changing jobs and going after the next thing I just did it.

My life is very different. As I said, I went from spending most of my day focused on the details of the lives of a set group of people (my students) to focusing on technical issues with my camera, editing words, and chasing down sources. I love it though. I'm in the zone when I'm working on a story and I feel great when I have a tangible product at the end of a day (an article or video). That is the one struggle I had with teaching—I knew I was making a difference but it was sometimes hard to measure. And my measurement didn't always match up with the school districts. Inspiration and motivation don't fit into a bubble on a standardized test sheet. … In any case, you want to have a job that doesn't feel like a job. I had those moments in teaching, but there were far too many other distractions that took away from the highs of being with my students.

If you're afraid to leave and pursue another career realize that teaching is a job but it's also a service. You give so much of yourself—your energy, passion, emotions, and mind—to other people. If you have nothing left to give or there is a fundamental part of you that desires change, you're doing a disservice to yourself and even your students by not going after it. That unspoken dream will lay dormant and transform into regret—why not give voice to it and be an example for your students that anything is possible?

Robin Asher's Story: From Teacher to Administrator and Back Again[55]

Robin's story is different than the other teachers who left the profession for greener pastures. She taught for ten years before leaving the classroom to become an administrator at a suburban high school in the south. Her story took a different twist when she left her administrative position and returned to the classroom.

The five factors that contributed to me leaving the classroom to become an administrator were:

1. I worked for wonderful principals at three of my former schools; they were all very good listeners, respected others' opinions, and were willing to try new ideas with their faculties. I found them to be inspiring.

2. One of my principals was extremely supportive of my entering the field of administration. He spent a lot of time talking with me about the positives and negatives of the field and I felt like I had a pretty good understanding of what was ahead.

3. I also worked for some knuckleheads—all of whom were male—and I was thinking that the administrative pool of talent could use a smart, fabulous woman like myself.

4. Both of my parents were teachers and there are many other teachers in our family. I had grown up hearing about the profession—and about how

awful/incompetent/unethical/ downright dumb administrators were. I wanted to try to make a difference. (Yes, this kind of overlaps with #3, but I felt like I needed to step up and try something different rather than being part of the administrator bashing that always seemed to come up at family gatherings.)

5. I love new challenges and … I have "itchy feet." I get restless for change after a few years in a position.

I was in administration for five years. My office space was in the district's central office building, but I travelled to all of the schools in my district throughout the week.

The top five factors that contributed to me leaving my administrative position were:

1. **Emotional exhaustion:** I was passionate about my work with the four departments and it was incredibly difficult to work in a district that did not truly value the electives. This was demonstrated by inequities in funding and classroom space. I was frustrated when one department appeared to get a large amount of funding and new equipment while another had its funding slashed without explanation. I was also discouraged when I saw teachers having to schlep their materials to multiple classrooms because their subjects were not deemed as "important" as that of other departments. When I questioned issues like this, I kept getting the same answer year after year: Maybe "we" can do better next year. Next year. Next year.

There were also countless ridiculous comments from other administrators and Board members about the electives and special programs. One of the worst was hearing a Board member complain about how the district had to spend money on special programs and classes for the English Language Learners. During a Board meeting, this particular individual said, "Why do we have to pay for these kids anyway? Most of them are here illegally, right? My grandparents pulled themselves up by their bootstraps and learned English on their own. Why do we have to pay for all of these special programs now?" Ugh. Seriously?

2. **Sexism:** Administration is definitely—most definitely—a boys' club. Sheryl Sandburg can talk, talk, talk about "leaning in" and such, but it was really damn hard. So many meetings would drag on because there were digressions about sports, fantasy football, golf outings, etc. We girls (the token female administrators) had to play the game and be polite through all of this chatter, but I was dying a slow death. I'm not interested in sports, I'm not interested in fantasy football and, honestly, I'll only run if there's a fire. However, to be fair, one administrator really tried to keep things a bit less male and sports-dominated … perhaps because he wasn't a jock/former coach himself. He tried the hardest to avoid that stuff and I always appreciated his efforts.

3. **Sexual harassment:** During my third year in the administrative ranks, two male administrators grabbed my ass at a Christmas party. It was a game of sorts to them, but not to me — I left immediately. They thought it was a big joke and probably rationalized it as, "Hey, I was drunk and stupid. No harm, no foul." One of them apologized later via a pathetic greeting card. The other did not apologize and tried to pretend it didn't happen. I confronted him about it and he finally apologized. I talked about it with a couple of female administrators and we agreed that I would never get anywhere if I were to "make a fuss" about it because these administrators had some buddies in high places. That was pretty demoralizing. I now have to work with one of these individuals and he is very cautious when interacting with me. I think I could ask for anything and I would get it—not that I would ever ask —because he knows that I'll never forget his "indiscretion."

I also had to tolerate a lot of comments about my appearance from the good ole boys. The female administrators' clothing and hairstyles were always up for comment by the male administrators. It was annoying and not at all flattering. I was there to work and advocate for my departments, not just be a pretty face sitting at the conference table. And, no, gentlemen, I will not bring in the coffee and cookies for the meeting.

4. **Crushing workload:** I oversaw four elective departments across three campuses, plus I had multiple grants and budgets to manage. I did have a competent secretary that I shared with a few other administrators; it helped to have her assistance, but I wished that she had more time to help with my multiple responsibilities. It was brutal. Absolutely brutal. The amount of work with teaching is not even half as bad — and you know that's saying something.

5. **Moral compass:** I always felt that the Danielson rubric for teacher evaluations did not allow for enough flexibility when evaluating teachers. The teachers in my departments were terribly nervous when they were up for evaluation because they knew that it was a tough rubric and that I would have to document everything. I always tried to be fair and to point out all of their positive work in the classroom, but it was tough. In my heart of hearts, I hated feeling as if I was screwing these teachers over when I had to give a "Satisfactory" instead of an "Excellent." It wasn't worth it. There is no specific descriptor on the Danielson rubric for love, compassion, and empathy. I was tired of not being able to recognize these important elements in my teachers' performance.

I also had weird things happen where material from my teachers' evaluations was 'borrowed' by building administrators. For example, if I evaluated a teacher first semester and then a building administrator evaluated him second semester, I would see phrases and sentences from my first semester evaluation in the second semester evaluation completed by the building administrator. So, in essence, I would do all of the hard work of coming up with just the right phrase or suggestion … and then the building administrators would 'borrow' them. This probably happened twenty times over the five years I was an administrator. I was tired of working with people who weren't smart enough or willing to come up with their own comments. The teachers in my departments told me about these "appropriations." They always picked up on it and would half laugh, half groan with me about how my evaluations were always the "originals" in their files.

I knew at the beginning of my fourth year in administration that I needed to get out of this particular administrative position. I have four young children and I didn't want a twelve-month job, so I looked for administrative positions that were nine or 10 months. I found a couple of nice options, but they weren't quite right. There would be issues such as a long commute, vague job descriptions, having to clean up major messes left by the previous administrator, etc. I finally realized that I was looking for a job that would be like teaching: nine to 10 months, lots of positive contact with kids, nice school, nice commute. I had my "well, duh" moment when I realized that I should just go back to the classroom in my current district and live happily ever after. The scariest part about leaving this position was self-doubt: I have two master's degrees, my doctorate is in Curriculum and Instruction, I am a Fulbright Scholar, I have travelled through Latin America, presented at multiple professional conferences, and I am an adjunct professor at a local college … but I was still so afraid that I would stink as a teacher. After being out for five years, I was nervous that I wouldn't be as good as my students deserved. I knew how important those fifty minutes were, particularly for my struggling students, and I wanted to do an excellent job every single day.

To overcome those fears I worked my tail off and asked my colleagues a lot of questions. Fortunately, I had a very good relationship with all of "my" (not mine anymore!) teachers and they were very kind to me. Everyone shared their materials with me and made me feel welcome when we shared classroom and office space. It demonstrated all over again how important it is to be a good person. I did everything I could to help "my" teachers when I was an administrator, and I was repaid in kind when I became their partner and colleague. I was so, so grateful for that. What goes around truly does come around.

In addition, I remembered fearing that I would be snubbed by the teachers outside of "my" departments. I was afraid that the teachers I didn't know as well would think that I was still somehow part of the "dark side" of administration and not a part of their teaching team. Luckily, I was 100 percent wrong. I found most of the teachers to be very kind and helpful and I always felt included. I did my best to mix with those who I didn't know well and to ask them questions about themselves when we interacted at faculty meetings and such. I tried to be mindful of the saying, "Those who are the loudest have the least to say," and to ask people questions about their children, hobbies, and general interests.

Returning to the classroom itself was not as difficult as I had feared. More than anything, I was excited to be working with kids again. I love teenagers and their youthful energy. However, while I was excited about my return to the classroom, I was always afraid that I wouldn't be thoroughly prepared for my lessons. I had done SO much research on effective teaching and I knew exactly how I wanted to do it—but it was incredibly time-consuming to get everything ready week after week. I was always afraid that I wouldn't be fully prepared, or that I would mentally give up and backslide into movies or meaningless worksheets. I wanted to be excellent every single day. My students deserved that.

My life is very positive now. I love teaching and I find it personally fulfilling and very satisfying. I love my students—and they know it. I focus on putting out positive energy every day in my classroom and I find it returned to me tenfold. This positive energy then comes home with me and I am a happier mother and wife. Yes, I have a lot of work to do and yes, there are bad days in my classroom sometimes. But, overall, I work with great kids and great colleagues every day and that makes me happy. Related to this, my parents live for five months of the year in Spain and they usually return to the U.S in late September. At the start of my first year back in the classroom, they said they couldn't believe how happy and relaxed I looked. I was not a stressed out, sleep-deprived workaholic maniac.

I can think of five administrators who have said to me in confidence, "This job is killing me. I want to leave it and go back to the classroom. You love the classroom, right? It was a good move for you, right?" And I say, "Yes, it was the best thing I ever did. Those five years in administration were tough and I'm glad I made the change." And they nod and act like they're listening … and then they never have the guts to "step down" and return to teaching.

I think this attitude of seeing teaching as a "step down" is the heart of the issue. Some administrators think that they are "above" teachers, but they are not. We're all equal, we're all working together for one cause: to make things better for our students every single day. One position is not "better" than another.

For the administrators who want to leave teaching, but are afraid to because of their egos are linked to their position, they fear the opinions of their peers, the reduction of salary and benefits (which was actually quite minimal), or the fear that they will not be able to do the job in the classroom … I have one thing to say: Just friggin' do it. Your ego can take it. Your peers' opinions are not important. Not having to get your suits dry-cleaned will be a step in the right budgetary direction. Follow your heart and go work with the best kids in the world in your classroom. You will do the happy dance every single day.

CHAPTER 10
ENJOY EVERY ASPECT OF YOUR LIFE

I**T'S INCREDIBLY EASY TO BECOME OBSESSED** about every little thing you do during the day, which means your job naturally spills over into your personal life. I thought I wasn't doing an effective job if I didn't grade every single sheet of paper my students completed. I felt I needed to grade papers at least four to five days a week which meant carrying stacks of papers home every weekend. I had my kids help me grade worksheets and record them before the days of electronic grade books. I wanted to be a great teacher and spent most of my free time doing just that. After signing my first teaching contract my main focus went something like this:

1. Do the best job possible, which meant spending every free hour planning lessons, grading essays and every single worksheet I gave to students, ensuring all yearbook deadlines were met and never, ever missing a day of work.

2. Being a great mom and wife, which meant ensuring laundry was done, the house was somewhat clean (I knew there was no way possible it could be spotless) and everyone ate 3 square meals and a few snacks every single day.

3. Attending to my kids' extracurricular needs.

You noticed than my personal needs failed to make the list because I was a guilt ridden mom who felt I needed to ensure everyone else's needs were met first and if there was any time left over then I could attend to my own needs and desires. Needless to say, that never, ever happened. I did squeeze in hair appointments and doctor visits when I really needed them but that was the extent of my self-care regimen. Since that time my life has done a complete 180-degree change. I no longer think I need to self-sacrifice my life to do and be what I think I need to be for everyone else. It took a long time, dozens of self-help books and becoming a life coach to finally understand that it all begins with me and I get to choose how I live my life and spend my days.

Shutting Off your Teacher Brain

In the last two years I've experimented with the idea of shutting off my teaching brain once I left work. This meant I refused to do any lesson planning or grading at home. There are a couple of times when I needed to break this rule because of impending deadlines, but I've been able to leave hundreds of essays that needed to be graded at work and use my free time during the school day to grade and plan and copy future assignments. It hasn't always been easy and I've tried to guilt myself into taking work home without success. What I learned from this experiment is that I'm now able to enjoy my life outside the classroom more than I've ever done before and it's made a world of difference in my quality of life.

I now have more time to exercise, take classes, hang out with friends, garden (something I really enjoy doing, thanks to a patient neighbor), read and, most importantly, write this book. There's no way I would have been able to do the research, interview doctors and former teachers and have enough energy to actually write the words you're now reading if I hadn't altered my priorities a couple of years ago.

I know this sounds blasphemous but really it's not. I realized that when I took time to do the things I loved outside of school, my life changed. I no longer dreaded Monday morning because I knew that Monday night meant spending time watching Monday Night Football—and quilting. Interjecting various fun activities into my work week helped me focus on school while I was there and I no longer dreaded dragging home stacks of assignments to grade. Of course it took longer to grade essays, but I was able to assign shorter ones that focused only on the specific skills I wanted my students to master. Doing this changed the quality of my life, and it can do the same for you.

Five Steps to Help You Live a Balanced and HAPPE Life

1. Put your wants, needs and desires at the top of the list. Be selfish for once without feeling guilty. I'm reminded of this every time I board a plane and the flight attendant tells me to put on my oxygen mask first. If your self-love tank is low how can you give freely to others what you can't give to yourself? Realize that it's OK to ask for help and that doing so doesn't make you a horrible person or an incompetent teacher. It just makes you an honest person who wants to set clear priorities.

2. Make a list of your top five areas of focus. What's most important to you? Which areas of your life give you the most pleasure? Then look at how you prioritize your time to see if you are truly living up to your list. Visit *www.sherylshields.com* to download a copy of the **Life Priority Worksheet** to help you see how you spend your time.

3. If your list isn't congruent with how you really want to live, you get to change it. What can you do to spend less time doing work (grading papers and lesson planning) at home and more time doing things with the people you love?

4. Once you've done number three, you get to make time to do those things. For years I was an avid quilter and then life got in the way. I started teaching fulltime and my stack of quilting projects just sat idly by, longing for me to complete them. Then September 11, 2001 happened. For the next few nights I watched the news at my sewing machine table. That gave birth to my Friday night quilting dates. It felt great to release my creativity again. Having something to look forward to at the end of a hectic week was a gift I gave to myself every week and it made a huge difference in reducing my stress levels.

5. Make plans to spend quality time with family and friends. Doing so gives you something to look forward to and releases Oxytocin, a brain hormone that produces that warm and fuzzy feeling you get when you do things you love with people you love.

Your Life = Your Choice

You get to choose how you live your life and what you do in your free time away from school. Incorporating the BE HAPPE plan into your personal and professional life can help you live a happier and healthier life.

You entered this profession to share your passion with young minds. The way I taught and talked to students changed drastically when I realized what a privilege it is to teach. Another shift occurred as I researched and wrote this book. I learned that I get to do this job and that by accepting that task I also get to bear witness when my students successfully master a difficult skill. I get to help kids learn and that's a marvelous experience. When I open my heart and share my love of teaching and learning, I secretly hope they will share their expertise as well. One of my favorite quotes from Maya Angelou perfectly explains what we do and how we should do it:

"I've learned that people will forget what you said, people will forget what you did, but people will never forget how you made them feel."

How about we set an intention to make every student that sits in front of us feel as though they're special and loved, and capable of doing the work we ask of them. When we come from this place of love and kindness, they can't help but do the same. I'm not saying it will be easy and some will never respond in kind, but those who do will be forever grateful. You see, every student deserves a kind and loving teacher. When you can't do that anymore, it's time to heed the yearnings of your heart and do something else. It's just that simple. Every student deserves to get a quality education from a passionate teacher.

APPENDIX A:
ELIMINATE BURNOUT

1. Why did you become a teacher or _____?
   (Insert your job title if you're not a teacher.)

2. What are the top five things you love about your job?

3. What's one of the best experiences you've ever had as a teacher or _____?

4. Are you excited, happy, depressed or anxious when you think about getting up for work each morning?

5. Have you thought about quitting within the past two years?

6. If you answered yes to question number five, how many times have you thought about quitting?

7. If you were offered another job outside of the teaching profession and you made the same amount of money (or perhaps even less) would you take it?

8. Why or why not?

9. What are your top five complaints about your job?

10. What can you do to solve the complaints you just wrote for question nine?

11. Now determine if you are feeling more positive (+1-10) or negative (-1-10) about teaching.

APPENDIX B:
TIPS FOR TEACHING TRAMATIZED KIDS

➡ **Help children regulate emotions in order to master social and academic skills.** School can often be a safe haven where these students learn how to manage their emotions and deal with difficult situations. Traumatized children operate at a high level of arousal and fear, making it difficult for them to process information. Anything that reminds a child of the trauma (a facial expression, the color of someone's hair) can trigger behaviors that may not be appropriate in the classroom. Teachers can learn to recognize when their trauma students are experiencing intense emotions so that they can refer them to the appropriate support staff for intervention if there's not enough time to directly respond to the student. This may be impossible to do in some urban schools where a large population of students may live in areas riddled with violence and crime. Knowing what triggers or motivates certain actions goes a long way in building a support system these students can come to trust and go to when they feel overwhelmed during the school day. Physical activities such as martial arts, yoga, and theater are becoming recognized as important activities that can help traumatized children reduce hyper-arousal and can be incorporated in various classroom activities to teach them how to concentrate and learn. Also, simple accommodations such as creating a safe space, or "peace corner," in the classroom; alerting children to any loud noises (e.g., bells, fire alarms) before they occur; and giving children goal-directed tasks that involve movement (e.g., passing out papers) can help children who are aroused regulate their emotions.[24]

➡ **Maintaining high academic standards**. It's important to set the same academic standards for trauma kids as you do for regular students. There may be times in which you modify the assignments depending on the extent of the trauma they may be experiencing in their lives. They need to be held accountable in order to learn important self-efficacy skills needed to overcome the effect the trauma has had on their lives. Children often interpret lowered standards as validation of a sense of themselves as worthless, a self-image created by the trauma. Ideally, it is best to let the student know that, despite the travails of his or her life, your expectation is that the student will continue to meet the high standards set for all the children, and that the school will help to make that possible.

➡ **Helping children feel safe.** Many of the academic and behavioral difficulties experienced by traumatized children are consequences of the persistent state of fear in which they live. For them to be educated effectively, it is essential that they feel physically and emotionally safe at school. Training should include discussion of how the school can ensure that abusive parents do not enter the building, how to make the classroom safe from teasing and bullying, ways to help children perceive adults as safe and positive, how to reinforce predictability in the classroom, and how to help traumatized children react to the unexpected (e.g., a schedule change).[25]

➡ **Managing behavior and setting limits.** Traumatized students must be held accountable for their behavior. However, a behavior-management system should be based on an understanding of why a particular child might respond inappropriately in the classroom and on the relational and academic needs of that child. Traumatized children may need to learn that obeying rules will make a positive difference in their lives; the experience of many children growing up in households plagued by family violence is that rules are arbitrary. It is essential to put in place a school-wide coordinated behavior-management system that emphasizes positive behavioral supports. In addition, traumatized children may benefit from social-skills groups that teach children what behaviors are socially acceptable at school, discuss ways to make friends, and help them learn to trust adults.[26]

➡ **Reduce bullying and harassment.** Traumatized students will particularly benefit from a predictable environment that is bully and harassment-free. To create such an environment, school-wide policies concerning bullying and harassment should be established and all staff and students should be trained in how to recognize and respond appropriately.[27]

➡ **Help children have a sense of agency.** Teachers can help traumatized children cultivate a sense that they can control their environment by creating structures within which children can make choices. Making choices strengthens one's sense of empowerment; having structured opportunities to make choices helps traumatized children overcome the chronic feeling of powerlessness that family violence induces. Learning to accept school boundaries and make appropriate choices within these boundaries can foster a much-needed sense of self-control in traumatized children who chronically seek to be in control of others.[28]

➡ **Build on their strengths.** Every child has an area of strength in which he or she excels, whether it is in academics, art, music or sports. When educators can identify and focus on a child's strength, they afford the child the opportunity to experience success, with all the emotional implications of doing something well. This is an important starting point in mastering academic content and social relations, which in turn can serve as a basis for success at school.[28]

➡ **Understand the connection between behavior and emotion.** Traumatized children are often unable to express their experiences in ways adults can readily understand. Lacking the words to communicate their pain, they may express feelings of vulnerability by becoming aggressive or feigning disinterest in academic success because they believe they cannot succeed. Moreover, they themselves may not understand why they are upset or acting out, creating a disconnect between experience, emotion, and actions. When teachers don't understand why a child is acting out, they are likely to focus on the behavior, not on the emotion behind it. Training should help staff understand that a traumatized child's disruptive behavior often is not a matter of willful defiance, but originates in feelings of vulnerability. Once teachers grasp this critical insight, they will be able to work toward responding to what the child may be feeling, rather than solely on the problematic behavior.[28]

➡ **Avoid labels.** Training needs to emphasize the negative consequences of publicly labeling children "traumatized" or "abused." Labeling carries the risk of making trauma into a prominent feature of the child's identity.[28]

APPENDIX C:
WAYS TO GET MOTIVATED TO EXERCISE

List five reasons why you're afraid to start an exercise program:

1. _____
2. _____
3. _____
4. _____
5. _____

Which one of the answers are you the most afraid of?

_____

What are you most afraid of?

_____

Why are you afraid?

_____

What would you do if that thought magically disappeared and never, ever came back?

_____

_____

What action would you take right now if you never, ever thought that scary thought again?

_____

_____

What small action can you take today to move you toward living a happier and healthier life which includes some sort of regular exercise?

_____

What small step can you take after that?

_____

Your job is to break down any negative thought that's keeping you from moving toward living your happiest and healthiest life. You can change your life by committing to doing one little teeny-weeny step a day toward living a different life.

This is how it starts:

First teeny-weeny step: Think of all the friends you know who have successfully incorporated some sort of exercise in their lives in the past few days, months or years.

Second teeny-weeny step: You call, text or send them a Facebook message asking if you can talk to them about how they started.

Third teeny-weeny step: Before your talk, write a list of all the questions you can possibly think of. Don't be afraid to ask questions you think are stupid, because they aren't. What you're really doing is seeking information so you can make an informed decision as to which gym you may want to join or who's a good personal trainer.

Fourth teeny-weeny step: Talk to coworkers, especially gym teachers for recommendations.

Fifth teeny-weeny step: Choose a goal and then set a timetable for attaiting it. It's also a good idea to set mile-markers so you see you're steadily moving toward your goal.

Sixth teeny-weeny step: Regularly reward yourself for attaining your goals. This is not the time to be hard on yourself. You know how your students react when you yell and try to negatively motivate them—it — doesn't! It also doesn't work when you lie and refuse to reward yourself for a job well done.

Your rewards don't have to be expensive or extravagant, although they can be when you finally reach your goal. It can be something as simple as eating your favorite meal or scheduling a night out with someone special or a group of friends. Once you decide you must do it or your inner two-year-old self will throw one hell of a temper tantrum the next time you try to make him/her do something s/he doesn't want to do.

Another good reason for doing it is because this kind of a reward program doesn't just work for getting healthier and happier. It works for all kinds of tasks. I use this kind of tactic when the last thing I want to do is grade a big stack of essays. I first decide how soon I want to have them graded and then I'll decide how many I'll grade at a time.

What I've discovered is that when I do this, and throw in a special treat at the end of each grading session, it doesn't feel like such a chore and I'm able to assess each essay more thoroughly than when I'm facing a huge deadline and they have to be graded in a few days.

Living a healthier lifestyle benefits you, and you get to choose whether you'll spend your time taking medicine for a variety of illnesses or spend that money doing things that add happiness and value to your life.

END NOTES

1 Moyer, Florence. "What Teaching Does to Your Body." Telephone interview by author. December 27, 2013.

2 Rademaker, Dr. Dennis. "Toxic School and How They Affect Teachers." Interview by author. April 29, 2014.

3 Giles M.D., Jon, Do Occupational Exposures Increase the Risk of Death from Systemic Autoimmune Disease? John Hopkins Arthritis Center, January 1, 2007, June 20, 2014 *http://www.hopkinsarthritis.org/arthritis-news/do-occupational-exposures-increase-the-risk-of-death-from-systemic-autoimmune-disease*

4 Delisio, Ellen. "Autoimmune diseases hit teachers hard." EducationWorld.com, 8 January, 2007. Accessed 20 June 2014 *http://www.educationworld.com/a_issues/issues/issues227.shtml.*

5 "The Teachers Who Say Their Classrooms Gave Them Cancer - BBC News." BBC News. June 17, 2015.

6 Arianna Huffington. *Thrive: The third metric to redefining success and creating a life of well-being, wisdom, and wonder.* (New York: Harmony Books, 2014) 4-5.

7 Litchfield, Dr. Robert. "How Stress Affects Your Heart." E-mail interview by author. March 28, 2015.

8 Singer, Jack, *The teacher's ultimate stress mastery guide.* (Thousands Oaks: Corwin Press, 2010) 11-12

9 Singer, Jack, *The teacher's ultimate stress mastery guide.* (Thousands Oaks: Corwin Press, 2010) 12

10 Fisher, Molly. "Factors Influencing Stress, Burnout, and Retention of Secondary Teachers." Current Issues in Education 14, no. 1.

11 Winfrey, Oprah. "What I know for sure: The Oprah Winfrey Magazine December 2008.

12 *www.mindgarden.com/products/mbi.htm*

13 Tugend, Alina. "Dealing with Burnour Which Doesn't Always Stem from Overwork." Dealing with Burnout Which Doesn't Always Stem from Overwork, November 29, 2013, Your Money sec. *http://www.nytimes.com/2013/11/30/your-money/a-solution-to-burnout-that-doesnt-mean-less-work.html?_r=0.*

14 Glouberman, Dina PhD. The joy of burnout.

15 Education Staff Health Survey 2014 Report *http://teachersupport.info/research-policy/research-reports/education-staff-health-survey-2014*

16 Markow, Dana, and Andrea Pieters, comps. "A Survey of Teachers, Parents and Studets." The MetLife Survey of The American Teacher, 2012. 45

17 Nazaryan, Alexander, "Pencils Down, Bottoms Up" The New York Times 21 January 2009, 28 June 2014. *http://proof.blogs.nytimes.com/2009/01/21/pencils-down-bottoms-up/#more-73*

18 Cole, Susan, Jessica Greenwald O'Brien, M Geron Gadd, Joel Ristuccia, D. Luray Wallace, and Michael Gregory. "Supportive School Environments for Children Trauatized by Family Violence." Helping Traumatized Children Learn, 2009. 127.

19 Cole, Susan, Jessica Greenwald O'Brien, M Geron Gadd, Joel Ristuccia, D. Luray Wallace, and Michael Gregory. "Supportive School Environments for Children Trauatized by Family Violence." Helping Traumatized Children Learn, 2009.15.

20 Cole, Susan, Jessica Greenwald O'Brien, M Geron Gadd, Joel Ristuccia, D. Luray Wallace, and Michael Gregory. "Supportive School Environments for Children Trauatized by Family Violence." Helping Traumatized Children Learn, 2009. 30.

21 Cole, Susan, Jessica Greenwald O'Brien, M Geron Gadd, Joel Ristuccia, D. Luray Wallace, and Michael Gregory. "Supportive School Environments for Children Trauatized by Family Violence." Helping Traumatized Children Learn, 2009. 35.

22 Finkelhor, David, Heather Turner, Richard Ormrod, Sherry Hamby, and Kristen Kracke. "Children's Exposire to Violence: A Comprehensive National Study." Juveline Justice Bulletin, 2009. 2.

23 Burke, N.J., et al. The impact of adverse childhood experiences on an urban pediatric population. Child Abuse & Neglect (2011), doi: 10.1016/j.chiabu.2011.02.006

24 Finkelhor, David, Heather Turner, Richard Ormrod, Sherry Hamby, and Kristen Kracke. "Children's Exposire to Violence: A Comprehensive National Study." Juveline Justice Bulletin, 2009. 53.

25 Cole, Susan, Jessica Greenwald O'Brien, M Geron Gadd, Joel Ristuccia, D. Luray Wallace, and Michael Gregory. "Supportive School Environments for Children Trauatized by Family Violence." Helping Traumatized Children Learn, 2009. 54.

26 Cole, Susan, Jessica Greenwald O'Brien, M Geron Gadd, Joel Ristuccia, D. Luray Wallace, and Michael Gregory. "Supportive School Environments for Children Trauatized by Family Violence." Helping Traumatized Children Learn, 2009. 55.

27 Cole, Susan, Jessica Greenwald O'Brien, M Geron Gadd, Joel Ristuccia, D. Luray Wallace, and Michael Gregory. "Supportive School Environments for Children Trauatized by Family Violence." Helping Traumatized Children Learn, 2009. 56.

28 Cole, Susan, Jessica Greenwald O'Brien, M Geron Gadd, Joel Ristuccia, D. Luray Wallace, and Michael Gregory. "Supportive School Environments for Children Trauatized by Family Violence." Helping Traumatized Children Learn, 2009. 57.

29 Katie, Byron, and Stephen Mitchell. *Loving What Is: Four Questions That Can Change Your Life.* New York, NY: Harmony Books, 2002.

30 Brown, Brene. *I Thought It Was Just Me (but It Isn't): Telling the Truth about Perfectionism, Inadequacy, and Power.* New York, NY: Gotham Books, 2008. xix.

31 Beck, Martha. "A Map of Change." In Finding Your Own North Star: Claiming the Life You Were Meant

to Live, 240-262. New York, New York: Three Rivers Press, 2001.

32 Troy, Cheri. "How breast cancer led to a happier life." email interview by author. April 29, 2014.

33 Need to reduce added sugar. *http://www.heart.org/HEARTORG/GettingHealthy/NutritionCenter/Healthy-Eating/Sugar-101_UCM_306024_Article.jsp*

34 Peet, Malcolm. "International Variations in the Outcome of Schizophrenia and the Prevalence of Depression in Relation to National Dietary Practices: An Ecological Analysis." The British Journal of Psychiatry, 2004, 404-08.

35 Farmer, Jill. *There's Not Enough Time...and Other Lies We Tell Ourselves.* Lake Time Press, 2012. 12

36 Farmer, Jill. *There's Not Enough Time...and Other Lies We Tell Ourselves.* Lake Time Press, 2012. 17

37 Farmer, Jill. *There's Not Enough Time...and Other Lies We Tell Ourselves.* Lake Time Press, 2012. 18

38 Farmer, Jill. *There's Not Enough Time...and Other Lies We Tell Ourselves.* Lake Time Press, 2012. 23

39 Hendricks, Gay. *The Big Leap: Conquer Your Hidden Fear and Take Life to the next Level.* New York, NY: HarperCollins, 2009. 159

40 Hendricks, Gay. *The Big Leap: Conquer Your Hidden Fear and Take Life to the next Level.* New York, NY: HarperCollins, 2009. 168

41 Hendricks, Gay. *The Big Leap: Conquer Your Hidden Fear and Take Life to the next Level.* New York, NY: HarperCollins, 2009. 169

42 Hendricks, Gay. *The Big Leap: Conquer Your Hidden Fear and Take Life to the next Level.* New York, NY: HarperCollins, 2009. 174

43 Hendricks, Gay. *The Big Leap: Conquer Your Hidden Fear and Take Life to the next Level.* New York, NY: HarperCollins, 2009. 176

44 Hendricks, Gay. *The Big Leap: Conquer Your Hidden Fear and Take Life to the next Level.* New York, NY: HarperCollins, 2009. 177

45 Hendricks, Gay. *The Big Leap: Conquer Your Hidden Fear and Take Life to the next Level.* New York, NY: HarperCollins, 2009. 178

46 Hendricks, Gay. *The Big Leap: Conquer Your Hidden Fear and Take Life to the next Level.* New York, NY: HarperCollins, 2009. 179

47 Hendricks, Gay. *The Big Leap: Conquer Your Hidden Fear and Take Life to the next Level.* New York, NY: HarperCollins, 2009. 180

48 Hendricks, Gay. *The Big Leap: Conquer Your Hidden Fear and Take Life to the next Level.* New York, NY: HarperCollins, 2009. 184

49 Totter, Michael. "Coaching others to tap into their original medicine." email interview by author. May 1, 2014.

50 Slim, Pamela. *Body of Work: Finding the Thread That Ties Your Story Together.* Kindle Edition. New York, New York: Portfolio/Penguin, 2013. 7

51 Leach, Kaitlyn. "Teaching all around the world" email interview by author. November 2, 2014.

52 Schulz, Christina. "Teaching in a bigger sense" email interview by author. March 27, 2014.

53 Wall, Josh. "The tough decision to leave the classroom" *Iamjwall.com.* June 2, 2014.

54 Alford, Natasha. "A new way of Teaching" email interview by author. July 2, 2014.

55 Asher, Robin. "From teacher to administrator and back again." Email interview by the author. July 2, 2014.

36965584R00107

Made in the USA
San Bernardino, CA
06 August 2016